THE NEW TEACHER'S HANDBOOK

Practical Strategies & Techniques for Success in the Classroom

From Kindergarten through High School

By Yvonne Bender

nomad press
a division of nomad communications

Nomad Press
A division of Nomad Communications
10 9 8 7 6 5 4 3 2 1
Copyright © 2003 Nomad Press
All rights reserved.

ISBN: 0-9659258-2-x

Questions regarding the ordering of this book should be addressed to
Independent Publishers Group
814 N. Franklin St.
Chicago, IL 60610

Design by Jeff McAllister and David Morin
Edited by Susan Hale and Anna Typrowicz

Nomad Press, PO Box 875, Norwich, VT 05055

Table of Contents

To my grandmother
Rose Scharf
To whom I owe my work ethic, curiosity,
and sense of humor

Acknowledgements

I wish to gratefully acknowledge the following people for their assistance in writing *The New Teacher's Handbook*:

Melanie Gaieski for many hours spent reading and reviewing, designing charts and forms, and offering advice on content and style.

Lauri Berkenkamp and Anna Typrowicz for editing that greatly improved *The New Teacher's Handbook*.

Charlotte Davis for reassurance, candid advice, and computer chart design.

Louise Gaston for review of troublesome topics and candid advice for dealing with them.

Marilyn Audlin for editing assistance, encouragement, and knowledgeable suggestions for content revisions and additions during the manuscript's earliest stages.

Yvonne Luken, Jacqueline Perez, and Bonnie Sutton for review of content and objective feedback.

Matthew Gaieski for providing a fledgling teacher's perspective.

Brad Foster for assistance as a computer guru.

Joyce Hansen, author of *Which Way Freedom?* for reading the earliest draft and encouraging a total stranger.

*"If there is any truer measure of a man
than by what he does,
it must be by what he gives."*

—Robert South

Introduction

What's in This Book That Can Help You?

"The role of the teacher remains the highest calling of a free people. To the teacher, America entrusts her most precious resource, her children . . . ."

–Shirley Hufstedler

What do you do now that you've convinced the personnel people, the local school administrators, and your friends that you really are ready to be a teacher? How do you prepare for that first class? What advice do you take? To whom do you listen? How do you keep from having a serious panic attack?

All beginning teachers have the same questions and concerns. They are all just as apprehensive about that first teaching assignment, even those who appear to be calm, cool, and collected. It may surprise you to learn that veteran teachers are nervous and somewhat apprehensive at the start of the school year, too. Experience has taught them, however, that they can alleviate their nervousness and assure a positive start by preparing in advance for their new classes. They know that the secret to success in teaching is in the preparation.

So, how do you prepare for that first class? What to do? Where to go?

Written by an educator who during a 30-year teaching career has taught students of all grade and ability levels, mentored numerous teacher-interns and first-year teachers, and taught graduate-level education courses, *The New Teacher's Handbook* answers these questions and many others in a forthright

1

and friendly style. The book is packed with candid "nuts and bolts" advice, practical strategies, and easily implemented techniques that will help you begin your teaching career successfully and avoid the pitfalls that discourage many new teachers. You can read *The New Teacher's Handbook* from cover to cover or use it as a reference to find specific information as the need arises.

The New Teacher's Handbook contains the following chapters filled with information essential to your survival:

1. *Preparing: Getting Ready for Your First Class*—Steps you can take to prepare for that first class before the school year begins.

2. *Observing: Discovering Your School's Power Structures*—Techniques for discovering a school's formal and informal power structures; viable strategies for working effectively with administrators, teacher-mentors, support services, self-proclaimed advisors, and others; and advice on whose advice to follow.

3. *Organizing: Arranging Everything for Optimal Learning*—Strategies for arranging materials, student seating, and classroom displays to create an environment that maximizes learning and minimizes behavior problems.

4. *Planning: Preparing a Teachable Lesson*—Steps to planning a successful lesson, techniques for assessing and addressing student needs and learning styles, ways to use common first day activities as assessment tools, and suggestions for assigning hassle-free homework.

5. *Teaching: Implementing Your Plan Successfully*—Tips for effectively implementing lesson plans; strategies for using plans as evaluation tools; and pointers for determining a lesson's correct pacing, proper development, and logical sequencing.

6. *Gaining Control: Preventing Behavior Problems*—Advice on teaching suitable lessons and having realistic behavioral expectations, developing educationally sound routines, establishing clear and enforceable rules, and anticipating problems to prevent them.

7. *Maintaining Control: Confronting Unavoidable Behavior Problems*—Strategies for dealing with unavoidable behavior problems by using positive peer pressure, creating an artificial shortage of something students want, isolating students from the group, forfeiting a favorite activity, using parental pressure, and obtaining assistance from support personnel and administrators.

8. *Communicating: Conveying the Right Message*—Methods of assuring effective communication with parents, administrators, and other staff members; strategies for holding productive conferences; pointers for dealing with angry or uncooperative parents; advice on what to say, how to say it, and to whom to say it.

9. *Documenting: Having the Write Stuff*—What to keep and why: information on how documentation can improve your teaching and the quality of students' written work, protect your career, reduce your responsibilities, and urge others to honor their commitments.

10. *Adapting: Bending Instead of Breaking*—Strategies for adapting to events such as sudden schedule changes, holiday excitement, unexpected new students, or impromptu lessons; information about accountability standards, certification requirements, and career realities; and advice about what to do if you are having trouble adapting.

11. *Persisting: Keeping on Keeping on*—Advice on the importance of persistence to career success and ways of being persistent.

Appendix A. *Some Answers to Beginners' Questions*—Practical solutions to problems encountered by new teachers.

Appendix B. *Sample Charts and Forms*—Examples of charts and forms that you can use to organize your classroom, document essential information, and learn about your students.

Notes

Chapter 1

Preparing: Getting Ready for Your First Class

*"One important key to success is self-confidence.
An important key to self-confidence is preparation."*

—Arthur Ashe

 **Chapter 1**

Case Study—The Confident Beginner

Preparation—A Key to Teaching Success

Learn About Your Students Before Meeting Them
Review Student Records
Speak with Those who Taught Your Students in the Past
Speak with the Parents of Your Students

Learn About the Curriculum

Learn About Your School's Policies and Procedures

Case Study—The Confident Beginner

It's the final faculty meeting before the children return to start the school year at Misty Harbor Elementary School. As the principal reviews the procedures for opening day, Kim Johnson, a first year teacher, listens intently. She's worked hard during this preparatory week and has done her best to get ready. She's learned important information about her students, the curriculum, and her school. She's memorized most of her student's names, contacted parents to introduce herself, decorated and arranged her classroom, organized her materials, and tentatively planned the first week's lessons. Kim Johnson is a little nervous but quietly confident. She knows she has done all she can to assure a successful start to her teaching career.

Preparation—A Key to Teaching Success

Experienced teachers know that one key to success in the classroom is preparation outside of the classroom. They spend many hours talking with students, parents, and administrators; reviewing curriculum guides; planning lessons; grading papers; attending workshops; taking additional coursework; and learning about their school district's policies and procedures. So if you want to be successful in your teaching career, expect to spend much time in preparation and realize that as a beginner you have much to learn and must use your time wisely.

Begin your preparation by learning about your students, the curriculum you are expected to teach, and your school district's policies and procedures. While information regarding curriculum and school district policies may be shared with you during new teachers' workshops (held before the school year begins or even several weeks thereafter), in most cases, you will be the one responsible for researching the information about your students.

Learn About Your Students Before Meeting Them

Before teaching that first class you must learn about the individuals who comprise it, and although this process will continue throughout the school year, you must begin it before you meet your first student. Learning about students before you meet them not only assures everyone's success during those all-important first weeks of school, it also alleviates, to some degree, your initial nervousness.

You can learn about your students ahead of time by:
- Reviewing student records.
- Speaking with those who taught your students in the past.
- Speaking with the parents of your students.

Review Student Records

Once you are given your class lists, make a beeline to the place in your school where the academic and confidential records are kept. Review each record and jot down information that might be helpful in planning for your students. (See page 160 for a sample Student Information Note-Taking Form.)

For example: Johnson, Jay—likes football, failed math, absent 30 days last year. Boyd, Mary—is a Chatty Kathy, homework completion inconsistent, supportive parents. Fletcher, Bill—easily distracted, hates to wear his glasses, collects baseball cards. Yarnell, Rainer—honor student, peer mediator, loves basketball.

Some of the information you write will be confidential so be sure to keep it in a safe place. Also, if it is extremely sensitive (for example, comes from juvenile services or psychological records), take the notes in your own personal shorthand to assure that, should they somehow be misplaced, they will not raise legal issues or prove to be an embarrassment to your student or yourself.

The time spent preparing for and learning about your students early in the year will help you start the year with extra confidence and save you valuable planning time as the year proceeds.

While taking notes, be sure to concentrate on what you are writing. Pay close attention so you can easily recall the main points. Don't let your mind wander to thoughts of the many other things you must do to get ready for the school year. The time spent preparing for and learning about your students early in the year will help you start the year with extra confidence and save you valuable planning time as the year proceeds.

As you hastily beat a path to your school's student records area, you may be confronted by an old teaching hand who says, "I never read my future students' records before the start of the school year. I don't want to prejudge them or create self-fulfilling prophecies." While the veteran's advice may be true for him or her, it is not true for you at this point in your teaching career. Unlike a veteran teacher, you do not have the experience to observe student behaviors and instantaneously select from several possible courses of action for dealing with them. Therefore, you must use additional research and planning to compensate for a lack of practical experience.

Speak with Those who Taught your Students in the Past
After you review student records, bolster your courage and make arrangements to speak with the teachers and support personnel (for example, counselors or social workers) who have worked with your potentially needy students (those who according to your research had past academic and/or behavioral difficulties). Be aware before doing so, however, that when a group of educators gets together to talk about former students, unless thwarted, they will spend that time exchanging cute anecdotal stories about their ex-students. So, if at all possible, try to meet with these people individually. Also, since the purpose of this meeting is to gain information about your students in an efficient and organized fashion, be prepared with a list of questions you would like answered. Be respectful of demands on their time, as well as yours, and try to keep each meeting to a half hour or less.

Ask questions to guide you in organizing your classroom and planning for the first few weeks of school. You might ask about academic and behavioral techniques others found most helpful in dealing with the child in question, whether they felt the parents to be supportive, where in the classroom the child might best be seated, who might be a good seating partner, and who should be avoided as a seating partner.

Keep in mind that you are gathering information to understand your students better and help them learn. You are not, however, obligated to use any of the suggestions that are given to you. Many times, experienced teachers state their "suggestions" so forcefully and assuredly that you might feel compelled to implement ideas that do not fit your teaching style. Such attempts almost always lead to classroom disasters. (See page 159 for an example of a Teacher/Staff Interview Note Form.)

Speak with the Parents of Your Students

After you review student records and speak with students' previous teachers, begin making phone calls to your students' parents. The purpose of these calls is to introduce yourself as the child's teacher and open the lines

Teacher: Hello, this is Mr. Wiseman calling from Highpoint High School. May I speak with the parent of Jaquan Wells?

Parent: This is Mrs. Cummings, Jaquan's mother, speaking.

Teacher: Hello Mrs. Cummings. This is Mr. Wiseman, Jaquan's science teacher.

Parent: Yes?

Teacher: I'm calling to introduce myself and invite you to contact me whenever you have any comments or concerns regarding his progress in my class. I noticed as I was preparing for my classes and reviewing records that Jaquan did very well in science last year.

Parent: Yes, he did. He really likes science and wants to be a doctor.

Teacher: That's great! I'm really looking forward to working with him and plan to keep you informed of his progress throughout the year. I hope if you have any questions about Jaquan's progress in science or any information that might help me do a better job of teaching him, you won't hesitate to contact me.

Parent: Well, thank you, Mr. Wiseman. I'll be sure to do just that.

Teacher: Thank you, Mrs. Cummings, and say hello to Jaquan for me.

of communication and support between the school and the parent. Because you will, no doubt, be a little nervous the first time you call a parent, jot down what you are going to say. Also, to avoid an embarrassing faux pas, you might ask to "speak with the parent of Johnny Jones" instead of Mr. or Mrs. Jones since parents and children don't always have the same last name.

Once you have introduced yourself as the child's teacher, you can ask about how the summer went and if the parent has any questions or concerns regarding the start of the new school year. During these introductory conversations parents may express concerns about the child's lack of progress in a particular school subject, or ongoing health or family problems that seem to be troubling him or her. (See pages 160–161 for examples of a Parent Contact Note Form and Phone Log Form.)

Since you are in the process of gathering information and building support to help you do a better job of teaching, do not mention negative information you have learned about the child during your student research. If the parent chooses to discuss something negative, listen and learn but quell the desire to say, "Oh yes, I read about that in her student record." On the other hand, be sure to mention positive information you have gleaned from student records. Comments such as, "While reviewing student records in preparation for the school year, I saw that Mary raised her math grade from a "C" in the first quarter to an "A" by the end of the year. She must be a hard worker!" will go a long way to building a bond with parents. If strong parental support is gained at the beginning of the year when students are fresh and the curriculum involves review, that support will continue as the school year progresses, students grow tired, and the curriculum becomes more challenging.

Consider making calls to parents from your school or use a caller identification blocker number so students and parents won't have access to your home phone number. Some teachers freely give students their personal phone numbers. They feel doing so assists them in learning about their students and gaining their trust. Think carefully before following this practice, however, since as a beginner you will spend many hours working with your students and preparing lessons for them, and you are entitled to what little time is left for some semblance of a personal life. When you give students your phone number, less mature students may decide to spend some "party time" making calls to your home just for fun. Additionally, lonely kids who need someone to talk to until mom or dad gets home may choose to spend that time on the phone with you. No one is suggesting that you not be supportive of truly needy children, and you might, after some very careful thought, choose to give a troubled child your home phone number, but you cannot afford to allow students to intrude upon your valuable down time. Experienced teachers who share their home phone numbers with students might seldom have problems as a result, but you must keep in mind that they already have strategies for dealing with those who abuse this privilege. If, however, sharing your home phone number is something you want to do, be aware that it could cause you unnecessary aggravation. The simplest way to prevent this from happening is to give students and their parents the option of calling you at school or contacting you through your school's e-mail system. (Should they do so, make absolutely certain that you return their call or reply to their e-mail promptly.)

If strong parental support is gained at the beginning of the year when students are fresh and the curriculum involves review, that support will continue as the school year progresses, students grow tired, and the curriculum becomes more challenging.

If you are a beginning secondary school teacher, you may feel that because your students are nearing adulthood introductory calls to parents are unwarranted and therefore a waste of time. In most cases you will find, however, that the extra effort taken to open the lines of communication with parents of secondary school students early in the school year helps you gain and keep their support throughout the year.

Since secondary teachers have many more students than elementary teachers and the time to complete introductory phone calls is limited, you may have to call parents of those students who may be potential problems first.

If you do so, be sure to call the parents of at least a few of the students who are less likely to be problems. Do this because word has a way of getting around, and concerned parents will soon conclude that you only called them because you thought their child was going to be trouble. Also, even though it is time-consuming, be sure to continue your introductory calls to as many parents as possible during the first weeks of school.

School budgets are usually limited so this introductory letter will most likely have to be sent home with your students on the first day of school. One way to be sure that busy parents at least glance at it is to provide a place for a parent signature as a tear-off and make the return of the signed tear-off part of the first day's homework assignment.

If you are a secondary or special area teacher with a high student load, you may find it more practical first to arrange a meeting with your students' former teachers and then to review the records of possible problem students. (Keep in mind that the impressions others have regarding your students may not always prove true for you.) Also, as soon as you meet your students and begin assessing their needs, you will want to continue reviewing the records of those students who appear to be having problems.

Learn About the Curriculum

If you haven't yet attended workshops or met with a mentor regarding the curriculum you are to teach, now is the time to find out some of the specifics. Ask your administrator or department chairperson for copies of

Sound Advice

If you are unable to contact parents by phone, write an introductory letter (with your immediate supervisor's blessing) in which you ask them to call you should they have any beginning-year concerns, comments, or questions. Be sure this letter is brief, well-written, and does not state unobtainable goals and objectives for the coming school year. Also, be sure it includes the school's phone numbers.

School Name
Address
Phone
Date

To The Parents of _____

Dear Parent,
I would like to introduce myself as your child's fourth grade teacher for this school year and encourage you to contact me whenever you have questions, suggestions, or concerns regarding his/her educational program or progress. The school's phone numbers are _____ and my e-mail address is _____.

Should you wish to arrange a conference, simply send in a note via your child or contact me at the above numbers. I will make every effort to respond to your calls and correspondence as quickly as my teaching schedule allows.

Since timely and candid contact between home and school is helpful in assuring a child's educational success, I look forward to communicating with you throughout the school year.

Sincerely,

---

the appropriate curriculum guides and teachers' editions of student textbooks and begin reviewing them. Pay particular attention to the types of skills your students must have before they begin this new curriculum or textbook. Next, find out how to obtain textbooks for your class. (In some schools textbooks are issued to teachers on a first-come, first-serve basis, and your students may have the threadbare copies with several missing pages if you don't put in your order quickly.)

Learn About Your School's
Policies and Procedures

Find out about your school's policies on such essential safety issues as student possession and use of drugs and alcohol, possession of weapons, fights, sexual harassment, parental child abuse, and so forth. Many schools distribute handbooks for teachers that not only detail the school policies on student safety issues and the teacher's role in carrying them out but also provide answers to several of the questions you may have about your school. (For example, How do I get supplies? What committees does the school have? Whom do I contact if I'm going to be absent?) If your school has these handbooks, be sure to get your copies, review them, and refer to them when necessary.

As the year progresses, you may find some teachers in your school don't adhere to particular written policies and encourage you to do the same. Should this happen, keep in mind that each teacher is accountable for following the written policies of his or her school and school district. Therefore, decisions not to follow policy can be unwise.

Chapter 2

Observing: Discovering Your School's Power Structures

"No member of the crew is praised for the rugged individuality of his rowing."

—Ralph Waldo Emerson

"Every society honors its live conformists and its dead troublemakers."

—Mignon McLaughlin

 **Inside Chapter 2**

Case Study—Team Player

Miss James, a teacher at Mills High School, has been called to the office. As she enters, Mrs. Henson, the school principal, greets her curtly. "Good morning, Miss James. Have a seat please. First, let me apologize for not taking the time to check with you sooner. The beginning of the year is always hectic for everyone as I'm sure you're aware by now. Miss James, we are happy to have you on our staff here at Mills and for the most part, are pleased with your start here. There are, however, a few procedures we need to clarify. It's come to my attention that you've had problems getting furnishings for your classroom. . ." Mrs. Henson pauses to read over a typed memo, "specifically a file cabinet and five student desks. I trust you now have those furnishings?"

"Yes, Mrs. Henson, I do. They were delivered yesterday and thank heavens, too! I've been waiting for them for over three weeks."

"I'm glad that your furniture problem has been resolved. However, if you have any problems in the future, please have the courtesy to contact either one of my assistants or myself before sending off memos to the area superintendent! Remember, Miss James, here at Mills you are a member of a team and that team is always there to support you when you need help."

Your School's Formal Power Structure

Part of your career survival depends on how well you understand and respect your school system's power structures. Every school district has a definite chain of command that is hierarchical in design. Since teaching is not an exact science, your effectiveness must be evaluated subjectively by those higher in the chain of command than you (for example, supervisors, principals, assistant principals, and department chairpersons). As a beginner, you are at the bottom of the command chain and cannot afford to alienate those above you by circumventing their authority. Unfortunately, it's possible you may unintentionally do so out of ignorance of the power structure or because experienced veterans (with their own agenda) might sometimes dupe you into "going over an administrator's head" under the guise of being true to your ideals and standing up for your rights. So if you have a problem and need the support of a "higher authority" to resolve it, first learn the chain of command and then make every effort to respect it.

The Role of Your School Administrators

Your administrators' most important role is to help you be a successful teacher. Because they are accountable for the quality of the educational program in their school, they must evaluate the effectiveness of their teachers. This means that, at times, they are going to observe your teaching, give critiques, and offer suggestions for ways to improve your lessons. When this happens, you must keep in mind that your administrators are not attacking you personally but simply assuring the quality of teaching in their school. As with teachers, each administrator has his or her own leadership style. Some are informal and democratic while others are formal and authoritarian, but all, regardless of their styles, want to see their student body do well and will support you in your efforts to make that happen. Also, since administrators are responsible for the safety, well being, and educational progress of hundreds (sometimes thousands) of students as well as staff members, they may not have the time to help you personally but will direct you to a staff member who might give you the necessary support.

Most administrators, in an effort to be helpful, tell their teachers (especially beginners) to feel free to bring them any concerns or questions they might have. In reality, principals and assistant principals expect their staff members to try to solve their own problems before asking for help. The questions you must ask yourself before taking a concern to your administrators are, "Have I tried everything I can think of to solve this problem on my own? What do I want my principal to do about this problem? Does my principal actually have the authority to do what I want him to do?"

For example, Jimmy Jones, an average student with average grades, has been a disruptive influence in your classroom since the beginning of the school year. It is now the middle of October and you have tried every strategy you can think of to get him to obey your class rules. You have conferenced with Jimmy. You have conferenced with his parents. You have conferenced with Jimmy and his parents. You have set up a behavior modification system and sent home daily conduct reports. Nothing has worked. Now it is time to set up an appointment to discuss Jimmy's disruptive behavior with your principal or assistant principal. You would like your administrator to agree to a conference with Jimmy, Jimmy's parents, and yourself. During this meeting you want your principal to tell Jimmy and his parents that the next time Jimmy disrupts your class, he will be suspended from school.

In reality, principals and assistant principals expect their staff members to try to solve their own problems before asking for help.

Your principal readily agrees to the conference but does not feel suspension is warranted. He feels the next time Jimmy is disruptive he should be sent to him. You are upset because you think Jimmy deserves a harsher punishment than a trip to the office. What you may not know (and your principal is not at liberty to tell you) is that he has been directed to reduce the number of male students suspended at your school. That being the case, he has offered you the most support he can at the present time.

It is always a good idea to take notes during a meeting with your principal and to review the contents of those notes with him or her before leaving the meeting. This is an effective way to assure the accuracy of your understanding of the material covered and solutions offered during the conference.

To evaluate the effectiveness of their school's educational program, most administrators make unannounced classroom visits, and any impromptu classroom observation, be it from administrators, supervisors, or parents, can be disconcerting for a beginner. The best way to be prepared for these visits is to teach every lesson as though it is an observation lesson. If, however, your administrators make an unannounced visit to observe your teaching, and you are unprepared, remind yourself that you are not the only teacher who has ever been in this very uncomfortable and highly stressful position, teach the lesson as best you can, steel yourself for some negative criticism, and try to learn something from the suggestions that will be offered to you. Do not, however, try to excuse your lack of preparation or go whining to other staff members about how unfairly you have been treated.

The Role of a Teacher-Mentor

Many school systems provide their new teachers with mentors, highly experienced educators trained and assigned to work with beginners. A mentor's role is to help the novice adjust more quickly and less stressfully to the realities of a teaching career. If you are fortunate enough to have a mentor, consider yourself blessed, and take full advantage of the opportunity to learn from a seasoned pro. Keep in mind, however, that you are the one accountable for what takes place in your classroom, and while your mentor may provide you with guidance and suggestions, it is your responsibility to use this information to improve your teaching skills.

Working Effectively with a Mentor

Working with a mentor is usually quite easy, at least initially. During the first few weeks of your career there is so much to learn and do that you will be grateful for any help and advice you receive. Anyone who patiently explains school procedures, helps procure necessary materials, listens to concerns, answers questions, and helps with initial lesson planning is going to be very welcome.

Problems can arise if the mentor begins making demands (regardless of how diplomatically) on you. You may find yourself resenting the person who reviews your lesson plans, observes your lessons, and always seems to find an area that needs improvement. (After all, you're not a college kid anymore! Didn't you successfully complete your teaching practicum? Wasn't your portfolio one of the most impressive the people in personnel had ever seen? Didn't your professors say you planned and taught some of the most creative lessons they had ever seen? So why do you have to tolerate this affront to your dignity especially from one who is so much older and obviously out of touch with what the kids of today need!)

To work effectively with a mentor, be mature, remain objective, and focus on the reasons behind the suggestions he or she makes. Teachers become mentors because they truly care about fledgling teachers and want to see them succeed and remain in the profession. Granted, each mentor has a personal style to which you must adjust, but this does not diminish the mentor's desire to see you do well or his feelings of pride, satisfaction, and accomplishment when you do so.

Here are a few guidelines to help you work productively with a mentor:

- Keep the lines of communication open. Your mentor isn't a mind reader and cannot help you if he doesn't know when something is bothering you. If you don't understand why he suggests a certain lesson modification, ask why. Also, keep those counterproductive feelings of defensiveness in check.
- Focus on learning what you don't know, not on impressing your mentor with what you do know. Be confident enough to ask him to teach a lesson demonstrating the proper use of a technique of which you are unsure. Observe the lesson carefully, take notes, and ask questions.
- Accept your mentor's help graciously. If he offers to teach the class, work with small groups, provide individual instruction, and/or prepare teaching charts, take advantage of his offer. Since he's "been there" himself, he knows when additional planning time and extra support are essential to your well being and teaching success.
- Recognize that you and your mentor are partners on a teaching team, and as such, you each have something significant to contribute. Your mentor brings advice based on years of classroom experience and you bring enthusiasm and fresh teaching perspectives.
- Avoid relying on your mentor to rescue you when you get in over your head. Make it your business to think of some alternative strategies for dealing with possible problems beforehand. For example, you are pinched for time and rush through planning an introductory lesson on similes. You know you should think more carefully about possible problem areas, but you know also that in the past when you've gotten into trouble your mentor has jumped in and helped you out. In your hurry, you fail to consider that the word "like" can have many meanings and uses, and as you teach the lesson, you find most students can't distinguish between the word "like" when it begins a simile and the word "like" when used as a verb. In an attempt to explain the difference, you offer a lengthy and rambling lecture on parts of speech and how they relate to similes that is met by blank stares and

loud complaints. In exasperation, you implore your mentor to help.

- Remember that although your mentor is an experienced pro, he or she is also a human being who appreciates genuine words of encouragement and thanks just as you do.

The Role of Support Services

Support services (resource teachers, guidance counselors, social workers, crisis teachers, and so forth) have definite roles based on their schools' needs. Learn about the various support personnel assigned to your school, their roles and responsibilities, and the procedures for getting their help. Introduce yourself early in the school year and talk with them about what they do. Do not demand aggressively that they provide services for a child. In some instances, doing so might cause them to move less than swiftly to meet those demands. Ask for help when you feel it is essential, but realize that support personnel are often forced to prioritize requests for services, so be pleasantly persistent and put your requests in writing. (See Chapter 9.)

To work effectively with a mentor, be mature,
remain objective, and focus on the reasons behind
the suggestions he or she makes.

Your School's Informal Power Structure

In addition to its formal power structure, a school has an informal power structure that comprises those who are respected by their bosses, those who are respected by their peers, and those who are respected by both. To avoid alienating the wrong people in this informal hierarchy, you must determine who respects whom. Do this by carefully observing the dynamics that take place in your school. Observe who serves on what committees, who helps with staff development programs, who volunteers for extracurricular programs, who arrives early and stays late, who arrives late and leaves early, who helps when there are problems to be solved, and who talks about problems but never helps to solve them, and so on.

*Remember that as a teacher you are a member of an
educational team, and as such, you must be supportive
of the other team members no matter what their place
in the educational hierarchy.*

Generally speaking, those who help with the logistics of running the
school, providing they do a satisfactory job of teaching their students, are
respected by the administration. Those who do their fair share of committee work, share successful lesson plans and materials, cover classes during
emergencies, and speak out about perceived administrative injustices are
respected by their peers. Those who help with the logistics of running the
school, are supportive of their peers, and can articulate staff concerns
diplomatically are respected by both their peers and the administration.
Those who work hard not to work hard and spend most of their time com-
plaining about all of the work they do are usually tolerated but never
respected by their fellow staff members.

As a newcomer, consider your school's formal and informal power structures before taking the advice of others. Be gracious when advice is
offered but discriminating when deciding whether to follow it. Advice
from someone higher in the chain of command must, at least to some
degree, be followed. Advice from teachers who are respected by both the
administration and staff should be seriously considered. Advice from
teachers who are respected by their peers should be considered but with a
degree of caution, and that given by those who are on the "outs" with the
administration should be considered, if at all, with trepidation.

When others give you suggestions about how to teach a lesson or discipline a class, they are speaking as teachers who have had the opportunity
to develop their own teaching styles, and while their techniques may work
well for them, they may prove to be a disaster for you. This does not
mean that you cannot ever use the suggestions of others (if so, this book is
a total waste of your time and money), but it does mean that the suggestions you choose to follow must fit your personality and teaching style. For

example, a soft-spoken five-foot tall female should not try to use the football coach's Vince Lombardi "give 'em hell" disciplinary techniques.

The Educational Team

Finally, remember that as a teacher you are a member of an educational team, and as such, you must be supportive of the other team members no matter what their place in the educational hierarchy. If another staff member is having obvious difficulties, offer your assistance. If you are assigned to committees and support duties, arrive on time, assist as necessary, and shoulder your fair share of the work. If you are not assigned extra duties, volunteer (when time permits) to help those who are. If all teachers are to be on hall duty when classes change, be sure you are on duty. As the year progresses and you gain more confidence, you will find many things you can do to assist others and create a positive atmosphere in your school.

Organizing: Arranging Everything for Optimum Learning

"Obviously, the highest type of efficiency is that which can utilize existing material to the best advantage."

—Jawaharlal Nehru

Inside Chapter 3

Case Study—Mr. Pool's Paper Chase

Placing Things Strategically

Design a Classroom Floor Plan

Create a Seating Chart

Cultivate the Correct Educational Atmosphere

Creating Problems by Over-Organizing

Case Study—Mr. Pool's Paper Chase

Mr. and Mrs. Reed have come to school for a conference with their son's teacher, Mr. Pool. They are pleased with Timmy's outstanding first quarter grades (his highest ever), and want to meet Mr. Pool, thank him for his work with their son, and discuss Timmy's overall progress.

Mr. Pool greets the Reeds warmly, removes a large stack of papers and textbooks from the chairs in front of his desk, and motions them to be seated. He reports that Timmy is working at grade level and making excellent progress.

Mrs. Reed asks to see Timmy's work portfolio, and Mr. Pool begins rummaging through a pile of folders stacked on the floor in the corner. "I've been meaning to get this stuff better organized, but haven't quite had the time yet," he says nervously, as he searches through the folders a second time.

While the Reeds are waiting, they walk around the room perusing the bulletin boards. "Oh, the Box-Tops-for-Books program ended September 30th, and I didn't send in my box tops. I'm sure I had enough box tops for several free library books. If I'd known the deadline, I would have made sure they got in on time. Did a notice go home about this?" asks Mrs. Reed.

"I think something went home," replies the distracted Mr. Pool as he continues his search for Timmy's missing portfolio. "I can't seem to find Timmy's work folder. Perhaps he put it in his desk." Mr. Pool reaches into Timmy's desk and pulls out a dozen crumpled papers with a large checkmark on them, several notices for parents, a half-eaten apple, several candy wrappers, and a bent up and torn portfolio folder.

"Isn't that something?" Says a perplexed and slightly embarrassed Mr. Reed. "Timmy's always been a very neat person."

"Unfortunately, untidiness seems to be a problem with most of my third graders," says Mr. Pool gesturing toward the many desks with papers and notebooks protruding from them.

Mrs. Reed has squeezed between a bookcase and a small table and is leaning across an office chair with a loose back looking closely at a bulletin board entitled Best Work of the Week. She sees three of Timmy's papers from the first week of school displayed there and asks skeptically, "Mr. Pool, do you have anything recent that relates to our son's progress? . . . and can you possibly find it if you do?"

Placing Things Strategically

"A place for everything and everything in its place" is not just an old adage but an essential survival strategy for the new teacher. Because time will never be on your side, you need to organize your student records, planning materials, and teaching supplies where they can be readily found. You must also organize your classroom in a manner that encourages positive classroom dynamics.

With the information gathered about your students-to-be as a guide, organize your classroom by completing the following steps:
- Design a classroom floor plan.
- Create a seating chart.
- Cultivate the correct educational atmosphere.

Design a Classroom Floor Plan

Because the classroom is (or should be) a dynamic place where students move around, you must develop a viable floor plan. This plan helps you seat students strategically and place materials to prevent problems as well as provide for maximum learning.

Before deciding on a seating arrangement, think carefully about the dynamics you wish to create with a particular configuration. (See pages 162–165 for some furniture arrangement floor plans.) Arrangements that seat students in clusters facing one another are conducive to group bonding and discussion and provide more space for movement throughout the classroom, while arrangements with rows facing the front of the room help focus student attention on the teacher, discourage unnecessary socializing, and require a bit more floor space. Many different seating configurations are possible, but consider arranging furnishings so that:
- Students can easily see visual materials presented during the lesson.
- Students with visual and hearing disabilities face the area of the room where the majority of the teaching takes place.

- You have easy access to student work areas.
- Students can move about the room without disturbing others.
- Materials are stored where their distribution creates a minimum of distraction to nearby students.
- Your desk is placed so that you have quick and ready access to all necessary teaching materials (for example, pens, pencils, erasers, chalk, staplers, paper clips, planbooks, or dictionaries).
- Chairs with writing platforms attached (the type used in some secondary schools) accommodate both right-handed and left-handed students.

Create a Seating Chart

Next, draw up a seating chart based on your student research and the guidelines listed above. Even though devising a seating chart may seem relatively inconsequential to you at this point in your teaching career, it is one of the most useful methods for organizing and controlling a classroom. Not

Sound Advice

Beware of Foragers and Hoarders

"Seasoned teachers" are often hopeless foragers and hoarders. If you arrive in your new classroom and find only left-handed desks, snack tables, folding chairs, and a folding table where the teacher's desk most likely resided, you are a victim of the foraging and hoarding syndrome. The trick here is to complain tactfully to the correct person so you gain some decent classroom furnishings. Whatever you do, don't point fingers at the teacher next door even though he seems to have a wealth of right-handed desks, cushioned office chairs, and two full-sized teacher's desks. Just go to the correct person in your school and calmly explain what furnishings are missing. As with any negotiations, ask for slightly more than what you need. While you wait for the furnishings to arrive (which, since you are the new kid on the block, may never happen during the current school year) make the best of what you have.

only does a chart help structure the classroom so that troublesome students are kept apart, students who work well together are seated together, and you have an aid to learning students' names quickly, but it also subtly informs students that you care about and control classroom dynamics.

When you draw up your chart, place:

- Distractible students away from high-traffic areas.
- Active students in areas of the room where they can move about without diverting attention from you.
- Right-handed students where they do not bump into left-handed students and vice versa.
- Chatty Kathies far away from other Chatty Kathies and Active Alberts away from other Active Alberts. (Opposites tend to make wonderful classroom seating partners unless they're love-smitten male and female adolescents, in which case, they should be kept as far apart as possible.)

As with everything you plan in teaching, both your floor plan and seating chart are subject to change . . . sometimes on a minute's notice. The furnishings in almost every classroom today are fairly lightweight and portable so they can be moved about quickly and easily. Once you feel more at ease in your role as a teacher, you may begin a lesson with the students seated in rows facing the front of the room, have them move their desks into small clusters for group activities, and then back to regimented rows to end the lesson.

Cultivate the Correct Educational Atmosphere

Now that you have arranged the furnishings and developed your seating chart, it's time to create a classroom that conveys (to an even greater degree) the message of who you are and what your expectations will be. You need to make every effort to ensure that your classroom projects the correct educational atmosphere. Be aware that the amount and type of visuals and educational charts you display, the colors you use, and the manner in which you arrange your materials give subtle messages to your students about you and your expectations.

When decorating and organizing your classroom, keep in mind the following:

- Bright colors create excitement while subtle colors have a calming effect.
- Many visuals (charts, maps, models, and such) placed in a small area tend to be distracting.
- Educational materials and student papers haphazardly stacked about the room convey the message that disorganization is acceptable.
- Tattered or outdated bulletin boards give the impression that carelessness is acceptable.
- Materials arranged on your desk in such a way that a barrier exists between you and your students give students the message that you don't want to be accessible to them.

Once you have organized your classroom, ask another teacher whose classroom seems to create a positive educational atmosphere about the impression your room makes on him. (For example, Does the classroom make him feel welcome? Does he think the room has enough visuals?) Asking for advice, however, places you under no obligation to follow it, unless the advisor happens to be your supervisor or administrator.

Also, don't be surprised if, once you are satisfied with the organization of your classroom, overly solicitous staff members offer you unsolicited advice regarding the organization of your room—advice based on their preferred teaching style and not necessarily the needs of your students. (See Chapter 4 for information on teaching and learning styles.) They may tell you that your room is "too regimented" and not properly arranged for "cooperative learning," or that you should allow your students to choose their own seats the first day of school and then make seating changes only if problems occur.

If you have read the preceding chapter, you know that this situation calls for tact. If the advice-giver is in a position of authority, explain that you have carefully considered many different seating patterns and have selected the current one because, based on your student research, it seems to meet the educational, social, and emotional needs of your students best. You might even interject some of your researched student information. For example, "You know I have Jimmy Jones, Mary Smith, Jarwan Hamilton, and Shernay Anderson in my class and according to what I've been able to find out, they are all good friends and they all like to talk, talk, talk. So I tried to seat them away from one another." If the advice-giver is not in a position of authority, do not feel compelled to defend the organization of your classroom; simply say you want to try this seating arrangement for a while before changing to another.

Creating Problems by Over-Organizing

As you strive to create a positive learning environment, take care not to become a fanatical organizer or incessant reorganizer. While a well-organized classroom enhances learning, one that is organized to the point of compulsion has the opposite effect. It's reasonable to expect that all thirty pairs of scissors distributed from the "scissors can" at the beginning of a lesson will be put back in the "scissors can" at the end of the lesson. It's unreasonable and counterproductive to refuse to teach a lesson requiring scissors because the last time scissors were distributed, one pair was not returned. When children are motivated and engaged in learning, classrooms tend to get disorganized and supplies and materials get messy and misplaced.

Also, at times, it may be necessary to reorganize your classroom in order to create a better learning environment. Frequent spur-of-the-moment changes, however, should be avoided since they create an unstable atmosphere and give students the impression that you are indecisive and weak. When this happens, they begin to question every decision you make and disorder and chaos soon follow. Reorganize your classroom only after careful thought and serious planning and not on impulse.

Chapter 4

Planning: Preparing a Teachable Lesson

"One does not plan and then make circumstances fit the plans. One tries to make the plans fit the circumstances."

—George S. Patton

Inside Chapter 4

Case Study—Mr. Sloan's Plan

It's the third Thursday in the month and "Teen Issues Magazine" day in Mr. Sloan's tenth grade English classes. Instead of their regular English lessons, they read and discuss articles in "Teen Issues." The students enjoy these lessons and so does Mr. Sloan. They are a welcome change of pace, and give everyone a chance to read about and discuss current teen concerns.

Mr. Sloan didn't write plans for today's lessons but had dinner out and went to a movie instead. It was late when he got home, he was tired, and didn't feel like writing lesson plans, especially since he really didn't need them. "Teen Issues" lessons practically taught themselves.

Mr. Sloan distributes the magazines and instructs his class to read over the cover story. The door to his room opens and the assistant principal enters. "Good morning, Mr. Sloan. I've heard such good things about you and your teaching. I thought I'd stop by and see for myself. May I see your plans for today's lessons for just a moment please?"

Planning to Succeed: The Steps to a Viable Plan

Now that you have learned something about your students and organized your classroom, it's time to begin writing some lesson plans. If you hesitate at this idea and want to make excuses for not actually writing plans, you will be joining the ranks of many beginners before you who have grumbled, "How can they expect me to write plans for kids I haven't even met? I can do a much better job when I can be flexible and creative. All I want to do the first couple of days is to get to know the kids. After that, I'll begin writing plans."

Because thorough planning is a critical component of successful teaching, lack of planning can (and usually does) prove fatal to many teaching careers. Occasionally, you might teach an outstanding lesson with little or no planning; however, the majority of the time poor planning results in poor teaching. So, if you want a long and successful teaching career, plan to plan. If you student-taught while in college, you have already prepared lessons for your cooperating teacher. Now you are on your own. You are the educational decision-maker. You must sit down with the curriculum guides and student textbooks and determine how to teach the material to children. You will need to make several judicious decisions based on your knowledge of the students and the curriculum they are to master and use this information to plan teachable lessons.

While planning a lesson can be daunting, there are some steps you can take to help assure your success:
- Review the prescribed curriculum.
- Determine what your students know.
- Determine the goal of the lesson.
- Teach the lesson in your imagination.
- Write out the lesson.
- Practice what you will teach.
- Assign hassle-free homework.

Step 1—Review the Prescribed Curriculum

Before you can begin planning, you must know the specific information you are expected to teach. Some school systems supply teachers with curriculum guides containing this information while others expect them to glean it from well-organized textbooks. If you haven't already been briefed on your school's curricular expectations, locate the necessary materials and begin reviewing them. Pay particular attention to the required units, the sequence in which you are to teach them, any additional materials you might need to acquire beforehand, and the prerequisite skills your students must have before beginning the units.

Step 2—Determine What Your Students Know

To determine this simply ask yourself, "Do my students need this lesson? Do they already know the concept or material and can they apply it correctly?" If you are not sure of the answers, you must use some type of objective assessment to find out. For example, if you plan to teach a primary math lesson on regrouping (borrowing), ahead of time, you might give students three or four subtraction problems that require regrouping. You can then assess from their responses whether the lesson you are planning is needed. To do this type of assessment you must think ahead. Since almost every lesson is based on understanding, if not mastery, of the concepts from previous lessons, you cannot sit down at the end of a school day (no matter how long and tiring it's been) and in a haphazard fashion think of something to teach the next day. What you teach and when you teach it is as important as how you teach it.

Using Common First-Day Activities as Needs Assessments

While your plans for the first few days of school must center around familiarizing students with your expectations and classroom procedures (see Chapter 6), this process can also be used as an assessment tool to gain information for short-term future planning.

Success in school (beyond the lower primary grades) requires skill in reading and writing and initial activities that demonstrate these skills can easily serve as "on the spot" assessments.

Copying Boardwork

When your students copy material such as a schedule or a brief homework assignment from the board, observe the following:

- Does the student copy the material quickly, accurately, and legibly?
- Does she use cursive or manuscript writing?
- Does she copy only one word at a time and seem to have difficulty keeping her place on the page?
- Does she drape herself over her paper so you can't see what she's writing?
- Does she immediately lose focus on the task?
- Does the copied material have many misspellings, omissions, and/or reversals?

As a rule of thumb, students who can easily copy material from the board are good visual learners (See "Everyone Has Style," page 39) with age-appropriate, far-point-to-near-point copying and fine motor skills. Also, these students usually have reading skills closer to grade level than those who experience great difficulty with this task. Conversely, those who struggle with copying from the board (again, rule of thumb) are not as adept with tasks requiring attention to visual detail, and have poorly developed far-point-to-near-point copying and fine motor skills, as well as below grade level reading skills. Since copying board work quickly, efficiently, and effectively is beyond their skill level, these students cannot successfully complete tasks that require them to do so.

Obviously, if the majority of your students can't copy easily and accurately from the board, you cannot incorporate activities based on this skill. No doubt, you will want your students to improve in this area during the school year, but you will not make the mistake of planning initial lessons with this skill as a prerequisite.

Remember that "on the spot" assessments only provide starting points to help you plan lessons for the first week of school that better match the learning styles and skill levels of the majority of your students. They are not thorough diagnostic assessments and can never be used in their place.

Completing an Interest Inventory

Have your students complete an "interest inventory," a list of questions about their favorite hobbies, books, sports, television programs, or school subjects. Aside from helping you learn more about a student and what motivates him or her, the inventory is useful for assessing a student's ability to express himself or herself in writing. (See page 167 for an example of an interest inventory.)

Advice

When evaluating the interest inventory, pay attention to the following:
- *Is spelling and capitalization correct?*
- *Does the student express himself in sentences or fragments?*
- *Does he answer in a few words or does he write a great deal?*
- *Are his answers easy to follow or do they go off on a tangent?*
- *Does the student use correct subject-verb agreement?*

If most of your students complete an interest inventory demonstrating writing skills commensurate with their grade level, you can plan their writing assignments at that level. If, on the other hand, they demonstrate skills on a much lower level, plan writing assignments on a lower level but resolve to improve upon those skills.

Reading Aloud

Have students read short selected passages aloud. These might include the class rules or procedures or a few sentences from a text. As students respond, take note of accuracy in reading and recognizing polysyllabic words. Do they read each word haltingly? Do they sound out words that should already be in their sight-word vocabulary? Do they volunteer to read aloud or do they need encouragement before doing so? Do they articulate satisfactorily or do they seem to have a speech problem? Your observations will help you assess your students' willingness to participate in class and the calibre of their word attack and word recognition skills.

If the majority of your class demonstrates word attack and word recognition skills at grade level, you can plan your reading lessons accordingly. If not, you must plan your initial lessons using reading materials written at a lower level and make more thorough assessments of your students' reading skills in the near future.

When using reading aloud as an informal assessment technique, avoid pressuring students to read orally. Some students are self-conscious about performing in front of the class, and putting them on the spot may embarrass them. It is better to tell your students you are going to call on them to answer at random, and permit those who don't wish to participate to decline politely. This technique gently prods those who are just a little shy and yet affords those really anxious about performing in front of the class a chance to save face.

Your observations will help you assess your students' willingness to participate in class and the calibre of their word attack and word recognition skills.

Listening to Learn

Give multistep directions and observe which children have difficulty following them. Can they easily follow multiple-step directions? Choose or design an activity that requires your students to demonstrate their listening skills further. For example, have them repeat a list of colors, names, or words. Observe who easily remembers what was said and who struggles to do so. Dictate another list, telling students to write down the items when the list gets too long for them to remember without notes. Observe who begins writing almost immediately and who waits until much later. This task helps to assess the strength and weakness of your students' auditory memories and provides a rough gauge of how much information you can present orally before they become overwhelmed.

Everyone Has Style

Your teaching methods form a large part of your teaching style, which almost always mirrors your learning style. Just as you have a preferred teaching style, each of your students has a preferred learning style. Some like to gain information by listening, others by seeing, and still others by touching and moving about.

The outstanding teacher adapts her lessons to meet the learning styles of her students while the poor teacher plans lessons that reflect her preferred learning-teaching style. Many times when a teacher says at the end of the school year, "That was the best group I ever taught. We worked so well together!" What she really means is, "That was the best group I ever taught. Over ninety percent of the class had the same learning style as my preferred teaching style!" If you want to be a successful teacher, you must plan lessons to address the learning styles of your students even when it means disregarding your preferred style.

For visual learners, use the overhead projector, the chalkboard, chart paper, pictures, computer, and videos; for auditory learners use the CD player, tape recorder, story hour, oral reading, and class discussions; for kinaesthetic-tactile learners incorporate student chalkboard activities, classroom "pass around" games, illustrating activities, skits and dramatizations or any other "moving about" activities that can be used practically in a classroom setting.

When your lessons include a variety of activities, you address a variety of learning styles and tailor your teaching to fit the needs of your students. By doing so, you assure that more students are successful and fewer are bored and disruptive.

If you want to be a successful teacher, you must plan lessons to address the learning styles of your students even when it means disregarding your preferred style.

Step 3—Determine the Goal of the Lesson

While this sounds ridiculously obvious, experienced teachers are sometimes stumped when asked what they want their students to know and do when they finish teaching a lesson. (For example, by the end of the lesson my students will know that multiplication is repeated addition and show their understanding of this using manipulatives, pictures, and number sentences.) You must think of objective ways to determine whether your students understand the concept taught during the lesson and can apply that concept correctly.

Step 4—Write Out the Lesson

As you answer the questions about the goals of the lesson, and any others you might choose to add to them, write out your lesson plan. Try to estimate how much time each part of your lesson will take (pacing), and how you are going to move logically (transition) from one part of the lesson to the next. If thorough planning is the foundation of a successful lesson, the mortar that holds everything together is proper pacing and logical transitioning, which are discussed in the next chapter.

Step 5—Practice What You Will Teach

Before you assign any tasks to your students (classwork, homework, tests, and so on) be sure to complete them yourself. Many lessons that begin well end in disaster because the teacher unknowingly assigns a practice assignment that does not apply the concept taught or is just too difficult for students to complete independently. So take the time to do the work you are requiring your

Teach the Lesson in Your Imagination

After you have a clear idea of what the lesson is to accomplish, teach the lesson in your imagination.

- *What examples are you using? What materials?*
- *Are you using charts? Are the charts easy to see and understand?*
- *What type of practice activities are your students completing?*
- *Are you distributing textbooks? How are you distributing those books?*
- *What are the children doing as the books are being distributed?*
- *What questions are you asking to develop the lesson? Do the questions follow a logical sequence to develop the concept you are teaching?*
- *What are the children's correct and incorrect responses? (It's important to imagine the incorrect as well as the correct.)*
- *What are your responses to incorrect answers? How are you clarifying misunderstandings?*

Areas that are out of focus for you will most likely present problems when you actually do teach them. It is better to replan a lesson than to deal with the consequences of teaching one that is poorly planned. If you teach a haphazardly designed lesson, you will end up with confused, frustrated, and ill-behaved students, and waste much time and energy revising lessons and reteaching concepts to an anxious and uncooperative class.

students to do. Chances are that if you get bogged down while trying to complete an exercise, can't follow vague text directions, or can't relate the exercise to the lesson's concept, your students will have even worse difficulties.

Step 6—Assign Hassle-free Homework

Of all the tasks assigned to students by a beginning teacher the one that frequently creates serious problems is homework. As with all other student work, homework assignments require satisfactory planning to yield satisfactory results. Because of time constraints, however, beginners seldom plan homework assignments with care and serious problems arise when homework is assigned with little thought to its overall purpose, content, fairness, and future evaluation. Sometimes school districts also exacerbate the problem by adopting homework policies that are idealistic and cumbersome and therefore disregarded by rank and file teachers. So before giving that first assignment, be sure to do your homework on homework.

Inquire about your school's homework policy. Ask the teachers at your grade level such questions as: How much homework do they assign? How frequently do they assign it? What types of assignments do they use? What percentage of students usually completes a given assignment? The answers to these questions will provide you with insight about the actual homework practices at your school and will help you avoid homework headaches.

The trick to quick and easy grading is to have clear and consistent homework routines and insist that they be followed.

Think Carefully—Assign Simply

Once you understand how your school implements its homework policy, keep in mind that homework should have valid educational objectives that enhance the instructional program. You might give an assignment to prepare for the next day's lesson, apply newly presented concepts, practice creative problem-solving strategies, or review recently mastered skills. For the first few months of school, consider assigning mostly review-type homework because it is the easiest to plan, monitor, and evaluate.

The simplest way to prepare review homework is to copy extra sets of a lesson's reinforcement or practice exercises and distribute them as review homework several days later. If your school's paper supply is limited, as most schools' is, you can accomplish the same thing by assigning practice exercises formerly completed in class as review homework. Although some might argue that this type of assignment is just time-consuming busy work, it does in fact provide review and practice of previously taught concepts and also invalidates the age-old student complaint, "I don't know how to do this homework. The teacher never taught us this stuff."

Making the Grade

While it's relatively easy to assign homework, determining if students have completed it satisfactorily can be time-consuming and frustrating. Without careful planning, the homework accountability and assessment process (ascertaining who did or did not do it and how well) can consume entire teaching periods and/or hours of your planning time or personal life. The trick to quick and easy grading is to have clear and consistent homework routines and insist that they be followed. One possibility is to have a specific place in the classroom where the homework is posted. When students enter the room, they are expected to put the previous night's homework on their desks, copy the new assignment, and complete a quick "warm-up" exercise. While the students are doing this, you can check to see who has not done his homework. This method works well only if you enforce it firmly.

Students who have not completed their homework can take forever putting their "phantom assignments" on their desks as they cajole you with pleas of "I know it's here! I worked on it for hours last night! Can you just come back to me, please?" If you weaken and agree to check back, you will soon find yourself running in circles around the classroom to check on assignments both real and imaginary as your class becomes more and more unsettled and time wastes away. The fairest solution to the problem of missing homework assignments is to place responsibility for finding and handing them in on the student. One way to do this is to record a zero for the homework, direct the student to hand it in at the end of class with a point deducted for lateness, and move on to the next student making it clear that the missing assignment may not be completed during class.

Once you have made a spot check to see if your students have done their homework (for example, have filled a page with some written matter), you are left with the task of grading it. Because this can be enormously time-consuming, especially when complicated assignments are involved, try to issue straightforward, easy-to-grade assignments. Stay away from homework that requires long essay-type answers unless you know from your "homework on homework" that your students write well enough so that you don't spend more time correcting their work than they spent doing it. (This does not mean you should avoid working to improve students' writing skills because it's time-consuming to do so, only that it is more efficient to work at correcting poor writing skills in class.)

You can limit your grading workload by reviewing a small number of homework assignments thoroughly each day and simply glancing over the rest issuing them a general grade (for example, a check or an S for satisfactory). Then make sure that on subsequent days you give all assignments an equal number of thorough gradings. Another technique to reduce your grading workload is to select a "student helper" to review homework. This student does not grade an assignment, but instead uses an answer key to check only those items that are correct. You can then review the incorrect ones, as well as any questionable items, and assign a grade.

The fairest solution to the problem of missing homework assignments is to place responsibility for finding and handing them in on the student.

Beware of Homework Quagmires

Two types of home assignments can produce serious complications for the new teacher and wreak havoc on her class: homework assigned as preparation for the next day's lesson and the creative project to be done at home.

Homework Assigned as Preparation for the Next Day's Lesson

Assignments requiring students to read several pages of material in preparation for the following day's discussion can produce serious problems when the majority of students does not follow through. Not only must you postpone and replan the lesson you had expected to teach, but also you must hold students accountable, enforce suitable consequences, and deal with less than cooperative students during the lesson. (In frustration, you're likely to lecture your class on responsibility and then have them do the assigned reading during class time, which has the overall effect of reinforcing the undesirable non-homework-completing behavior.) So, it's best not to use this type of assignment until after the first few weeks of school, and when you do use it, have a backup plan.

Creative Project Assignments

Occasionally, long-term projects such as creating dioramas, mobiles, models, or relief maps are assigned as homework. These creative assignments hold the potential for increased student enthusiasm and understanding, but if you don't implement them carefully, they can easily nullify student learning and positive parent-teacher relations, as well as cloud your objectivity. To consider some of the problems such assignments present and formulate some possible strategies for dealing with them, ask yourself the following questions:

Do all students have access to the necessary materials?

When students do not have access to the extra books, magazines, newspapers, paint, tagboard, scissors, glue, paste, crayons, and so on to complete an assignment, it is unfair to make the work mandatory. If the assignment is mandatory, you have the option of providing students with the supplies they will need, modifying the assignment to include materials they have readily available, or permitting them to choose an alternative assignment. Needless to say, you must handle the problem of lack of materials with great sensitivity since it may embarrass some students.

How will the project be evaluated?

Give careful thought to evaluation criteria and how you might avoid possible assessment problems. Determine if you will grade an assignment equally on content, neatness, creativity, and so on, and if you will give more weight to certain criteria. For example, it's possible for a student to create a beautiful relief map of South America and support his work with only a five-word written explanation. Once you determine the evaluation criteria, review them carefully with your students and send a copy home to be reviewed and signed by parents. Finally, formulate some strategies for dealing with problems such as requests for extensions; projects destroyed on the way to school or, worse yet, while at school; and students who obviously put forth little or no effort to complete the assignment.

Because creative projects arouse much interest and excitement, devise a plan for sharing projects with the entire class, and consider making these presentations part of your evaluation criteria. For instance, each student might give a short talk to explain what was done, why it was done, and what was learned while doing it. Students would then earn a "presentation grade" based on the number of topics they covered and how well they did so. You must control student presentations with enforced time limits as well as guidelines for the speaker's performance and listeners' behavior, or such presentations can easily decline into time-wasting, disorganized, non-educational, social events.

The overly helpful parent, grandparent, or adult family friend who insists on doing a child's assignment for him can pose additional problems when you attempt to evaluate a project. When the work has clearly been completed by an overzealous adult, you face a serious dilemma in evaluating it. (For example, the third grade student who lacks the fine motor skills to tie his shoes or cut paper along a dotted line submits a perfect scale model of a log cabin complete with tiny historically correct furnishings.) If you assign the project an unsatisfactory grade, you may find yourself facing angry and insulted parents. If you assign a satisfactory grade, you are setting an unfair, unattainable, and demoralizing standard for your students. Using the log cabin example, the average third grader cannot compete on an academic level with the average adult and should not feel compelled to do so.

Prevention through careful planning is the easiest way to manage homework problems. Prepare specific and diplomatically worded guidelines to explain and justify a homework project's parameters as well as to delineate the amount and type of help others may provide. If a parent ignores your guidelines and is adamant that special consideration be given to her child or insists on providing more than reasonable help with the child's work, your best course of action as a beginner is to seek an administrator's experience, judgment, and support.

The Teachable Plan

You have at this point prepared a plan that addresses the educational needs of your students, presents material at their current skills levels, allows for their various learning styles, and prevents homework headaches. You now have a teachable plan. The next step is to implement that plan effectively.

Chapter 5

Teaching: Implementing Your Plan Successfully

"It is not good enough for things to be planned—they still have to be done; for the intention to become a reality, energy has to be launched into operation."

—Pir Vilayat Khan

 **Chapter 5**

Case Study—Mr. Marks Works His Plan

Mr. Marks is concerned about the math lesson he must teach on division by fractions. He knew this lesson was coming and has thought carefully about how to present it logically. He has talked with other teachers who have taught the concept before and has also designed some hands-on activities to demonstrate the calculation procedure.

He begins the lesson with a review and moves through each of the steps deliberately and systematically. He refers to his written plan when necessary, asks questions to develop the lesson logically and sequentially, listens carefully to his students' responses, and clarifies points of confusion. His students grasp the concept with little difficulty and are pleased with their accomplishment, but not nearly as pleased as Mr. Marks is with his.

Plan Your Work. Work Your Plan.

While thorough and realistic planning provides the foundation for a successful lesson, a superior plan does not guarantee a superior lesson. Without proper implementation even the best plan will fail.

The following steps will help you implement your plan successfully.
- Use your plan.
- Move at the correct pace.
- Develop the lesson clearly.

Use Your Plan

Because you are new to teaching, remember to refer to your plan as you teach. By doing so you will be less likely to omit an important part of your lesson and you will also demonstrate to your students that you have developed a plan beneficial to them and are working to achieve it.

Write brief notes on your plan either during the lesson or as soon as possible afterward about what worked and what didn't. (For example, everyone was enthusiastic during review activity, but motivational activity stank, no one was motivated, kids were confused by the examples used to show the difference between communism and socialism.) Also write down notes regarding unusual student behaviors. For example, Jarwan had no glasses, Maria was asleep from 10:00 to 10:15, Ricki was very irritable, Meredith has worn the same clothing for the past three days. This may seem like a lot to do in addition to teaching the lesson and maintaining order, but keep in mind that your notes, no matter how minimal, can be used not only to assist you in planning and teaching effective lessons, but also as documentation that a student is having some serious problems and might need additional support.

The notes you make on your lesson plan can help you answer such questions as:

- Were the majority of my students involved in the lesson?
- During what parts of the lesson did students participate the most? The least?
- Did students ask clarifying questions? At what points did they do so?
- What parts of the lesson seemed to confuse students the most?
- What activities engaged the greatest number of students? The least number?
- Which students completed which activities quickly? Slowly?
- Which students seemed to have difficulty learning, and it was not caused by the quality of my planning/teaching?

Using your plan as a teaching tool is a good first step toward becoming an effective teacher; however, effective teaching also requires that lessons be correctly paced, skillfully developed, and logically sequenced.

Move at the Correct Pace: Timing is Everything

Pacing is the speed at which a lesson is taught. Correct pacing helps students to remain focused throughout the lesson. Pacing that is too slow allows attention to wander, dampens enthusiasm, and curtails understanding, while pacing that is too fast causes confusion and creates feelings of frustration and anxiety. A well-planned, properly paced lesson keeps students attentive, constructively involved, out of trouble, and most importantly, learning effectively and efficiently.

Skillful pacing is based on careful observation combined with good judgment; in some ways it could be compared to skillful driving.

Beware of the Beginner's Pacing Problems

Because of initial nervousness, you may tend to rush through lessons leaving lots of "empty time" at the end. When this "empty time" with its resulting student pandemonium (thirty kids with nothing to do but talk, joke, and perform for one another) occurs at the end of several lessons, you realize you must "do something" to avoid this down time at the end of your lessons. You may then attempt to slow down the lessons by belaboring the obvious. (For example, "Jovan, Mary, and Tim all say we should find the least common denominator to solve this problem. Does anyone else have another idea? What do you think, Juanita? So you agree also? How about you, Brian?") Alternatively, you may try extending the time it takes to get ready for an activity, which allows large chunks of time for preparations such as clearing off desks, distributing/collecting materials, or locating previously completed assignments. Such stalling techniques simply cause unfocused and unruly behavior throughout the lesson.

Determine the Correct Pace

Since pacing must vary from lesson to lesson, day to day, class to class, and student to student, no magic formula for determining good pacing exists. Skillful pacing is based on careful observation combined with good judgment; in some ways it could be compared to skillful driving.

A skillful driver knows when to slow down and speed up. She plans a route that takes her to her destination with a minimum of detours, stops, starts, and turns. She looks far ahead to prepare for future problems so she won't have to slam on the brakes suddenly, but she is ready to do so if necessary. She doesn't move at a snail's pace when the traffic is moving rapidly, or move at breakneck speed when the traffic is moving slowly. She doesn't jump from lane to lane leaving other drivers angry and frustrated from trying to determine where she is going next. She doesn't waste precious energy with jackrabbit starts followed by bone-jarring stops. She accelerates slowly, but once up to the maximum allowable speed, she stays there . . . traffic and road conditions permitting.

Likewise, a skillful teacher plans a lesson to achieve specific goals as directly as possible. Carefully observe the actions and reactions of your students, so you will know when to slow down and when to speed up. As you teach, think ahead to prepare for and avoid possible confusion. Do not slow down your students when they are capable of moving faster nor move in such a rapid and fragmented fashion that they become frustrated and angry.

You can achieve skillful pacing by observing the dynamics taking place as the lesson develops and by adjusting the speed of your teaching to direct, match, or control those dynamics. If, for example, the majority of students has completed a practice assignment and is having a "gab fest," it's time to move on. (In fact, the "proficient pacer" will move on long before everyone starts talking.) On the other hand, if the majority of students is still following the first direction when you are presenting direction number four, it's time to slow down. In addition, it's a good idea to add a few optional practice or enrichment activities to your lesson plan for those times when you find you've taught the lesson in record time.

 Advice

Not Too Fast, Not Too Slow

As a general rule, if students can chat among themselves and still manage to "stay with" the lesson, the pacing is too slow. Conversely, if students are constantly asking redundant questions and your first thought is, "They're just not paying attention!" it may well be that you are setting too fast a pace.

The elementary school teacher who invariably takes two hours to teach a one-hour lesson has a pacing problem as does the secondary school teacher who continually carries over and completes one day's lesson on the next day and/or shouts out the final main points of her lesson over the din created by her students as they pack up their materials to move to the next class.

In addition to your concerns about your students when trying to pace lessons correctly, you must deal with predetermined time limits (often set by curriculum guidelines) that require you to make critical decisions about what activities to add or delete from a lesson while still achieving its goals. Therefore, if students need an extra ten minutes of practical examples in order to understand better "the law of supply and demand," you must adjust accordingly and consolidate or delete parts of the lesson so the main concept is mastered within the allotted time constraints. The decision about what to consolidate or delete cannot be made on a whim but must be based on the instructional needs of the class.

Avoid Pacing Problems

First, understand that proper pacing is a difficult skill to master especially if your class has high ability students mixed with average ability students mixed with low ability students. Next, be sure to complete all of your student research. Then, focus on your students as you teach and make every effort to observe their actions and reactions. Look at the entire class, not just a select few. Be aware that, in general, right-handed teachers tend to focus more on the right side of the classroom leaving the left side out of their observations while left-handers do the reverse. Try to make a practice of calling on students who are not volunteering in order to determine if the majority does in fact understand the main points of the lesson and is ready to move on. (This technique can be used only if a positive learning atmosphere has been established. See Chapter 6 for suggestions about accomplishing this.) Finally, if it's apparent from the looks on their faces that students are confused, stop and ask about the cause of their confusion. If they can't articulate the problem, you probably need to back up a few steps and re-explain or reintroduce the concept.

Student Needs Won't Always Set the Pace

Ideally, pacing decisions are based on student needs, but in reality logistics can strongly influence the overall pacing of lessons.

- Time constraints set by curriculum guides—"This third grade science unit, Machines at Their Simplest, is to be introduced, taught, and assessed in fourteen one-hour, hands-on, discovery-method lessons."
- Problems with shared materials—Materials must be shared with other classes and therefore are available for a predetermined time period.
- School emergencies—Cancellations due to inclement weather.
- School activities—Assemblies, special programs.
- Your illness.

Unfortunately, where the logistics of running a school are concerned, you are often forced to practice a type of "pacing triage" where the needs of the many take precedence over the needs of the few. At such times, you must base as much of your pacing as possible on the needs of your students while being fully aware that outside influences are forcing you to make difficult compromises.

Develop the Lesson Clearly: Help Your Students Get the Picture

A lesson's development consists of the amount, complexity, and sequence of steps taken to help students understand a concept. To determine how many steps are necessary and how challenging each must be, you must complete your student research and a needs assessment. This information will help you predict some of the difficulties your students might encounter as they learn a particular concept.

The Learning Ladder: Steps to Understanding (More or Less)

You can view a lesson's development by picturing each piece of information necessary for student understanding as a rung on a ladder and the student as the climber. Students with weak prerequisite skills, limited ability, and/or poor self-confidence cannot climb higher because they find even one rung too big a step to take and need additional rungs. (For such students, you need to break up the lesson into smaller, easier-to-manage steps and incorporate additional examples and exercises.) Students with strong prerequisite skills and confidence in their ability to learn move quickly up the ladder, at times skipping several rungs while making their way upward. Sometimes these "quick climbers" ascend very high, look around, get confused, and need some rungs added underneath them because they really didn't understand just how high they were or how they had gotten there.

As a teacher your job is to add or remove rungs to increase and improve student understanding. You may have to break down complex concepts into their smallest incremental parts so all students have a chance to understand them. You can do this by completing the task(s) you want your students to complete and noting all the steps required to do so.

If, for example, you plan to teach division by two place divisors, your students must be able to divide, estimate, multiply, subtract, use good visual and spatial organizational skills (so they can keep all of the columns reasonably straight and all of the numbers in their proper places), and tolerate frustration (so they won't tear up their paper when they erase a hole in it after they have estimated too high or too low a dividend for the second or third time).

When this concept is introduced, some students will easily understand the theory, master its application, and move quickly up the learning ladder possibly skipping several rungs at a time, some will not actually understand the theory but will master the mechanics and move rather haltingly from rung to rung, and some will be unable to move up the learning ladder until you add rungs by taking them slowly and deliberately through each step demonstrating to them that they have the computational skills necessary to complete the task successfully.

Logical Sequencing: It's Just One Thing After Another

Not only must you know when to add or delete steps to help your students learn, you must also arrange those steps in logical order. If you wish to teach your class that vowels are a, e, i, o, u and sometimes y but start by giving examples of words that begin with the vowel i, followed by examples of words that begin with u, e, o, a, and y, respectively, you are not presenting the material in a sequence your students can easily follow or apply. The same would be true if you are a physical education teacher presenting an explanation of volleyball rules that begins with scoring, jumps to serving techniques, moves back to scoring, moves on to proper player rotation, follows with court dimensions, continues with a short history of the game, and ends with an explanation of the role of each player. In both cases you have failed to sequence the steps properly in your lesson so students can understand and follow the progression.

A skillful teacher sequences lessons to progress from easy to difficult using her students' current knowledge as the starting point. For example, a lesson introducing adverbs might have the following sequence:

1. Conduct a short review of verbs.
2. Have students underline all of the verbs in a paragraph.
3. Have students circle words near the verbs that they feel "add to" the verbs.
4. Review and discuss the students' choices stressing the similarities among the words which "add to" the verbs.
5. Arrive at a definition for adverb.
6. Practice by adding adverbs to a list of verbs.
7. Assess the students' understanding by having them improve some text by adding adverbs and/or writing a short "action composition" making use of action-enhancing adverbs.

Be Sure You Know Your Stuff

In order to teach a subject to someone, you must understand it yourself, so don't ever, ever, ever, try to teach a concept you don't understand or a skill you haven't mastered. The surest way to create student frustration and classroom pandemonium is to offer some convoluted, totally incomprehensible, obfuscating explanation of a concept you haven't mastered and don't understand. If you try mightily to understand a lesson well enough to teach it and still cannot, don't feel embarrassed about seeking clarification from an experienced colleague who has taught that concept many times before.

Chapter 6

Gaining Control: Preventing Behavior Problems

"Speak softly, and carry a big stick; you will go far."

—Theodore Roosevelt

Case Study—A Tale of Two Beginners

It's a Friday afternoon in late September at Urbana Public Middle School. Mr. K., a first year teacher, is teaching a lesson to his eighth grade Principles of Democracy class.

"Does anyone want to read the objective for today's lesson?" he asks.

"No!" someone whispers from one of the groups seated near the back of the room. The class breaks into laughter and students begin to talk among themselves.

Mr. K., unsure about how to respond, ignores the behavior, and, seeing no voluntary hands in the air, calls on a student at random. "Joe, read the objective for us, please?"

"Joe's not here today," someone says. Mr. K. makes a mental note to be sure to take attendance before the class ends.

"Okay, James, how about you reading the objective for us?"

"Kevin!" The student responds indignantly. "My name is Kevin! You've been callin' me James every day, and every day I tell you my name is Kevin." (More laughter and chatter from the groups of students.)

"I'm sorry, Kevin. . . for some reason I guess you remind me of a James," Mr. K. blurts out amid even more laughter and student chatter. "Well, Kevin, how about reading the objective for us?"

"I'd rather you call on someone else," Kevin replies politely. (More laughter and chatter.)

"Well, read it anyway!"

"But you said that if you called on us and we didn't want to answer, all we had to do was decline politely! I'm declining politely!" (More laughter accompanied by hands thumping on desks in, "boy-that-was-a-good-one" fashion.)

Mr. K. lashes out angrily. "All right, that's enough! I've had it with this class! You're supposed to be eighth graders, but you act more like babies! You've wasted ten minutes just over the objective. There's no point in my trying to teach you anything!" he rants as his students stare at him in amazement. "Take out your textbooks, turn to chapter 4, and study the material on the Bill of Rights carefully because you're going to have a test on it on Monday."

The class erupts in angry protests, "He's just getting even 'cause he's mad!" . . . "This chapter's thirty pages. I can't learn all this stuff in twenty minutes. I'm going away this weekend and won't have time to study this stuff!" . . .

Mr. K. stands dejectedly at the back of the room praying for the class to end.

After dismissal, he sits in his classroom trying to figure out how he got off to such a terrible start. He's a bright guy. He graduated with a 3.85 GPA, and got rave reviews as a student teacher, and yet now that he has his own classes, he's having problems.

The first few days of school went well enough. The kids seemed to enjoy coming to his class. They liked that in his class they could sit next to their friends and had to obey only rules and procedures they formulated. But after the first week or so, their behavior started to get out of hand. They talked to their friends when they should have been listening. They left the room to use the lavatory at the exact moment he was presenting an important concept. (Their rule stated they could use the lavatory one at a time whenever they "needed" provided they did not disrupt the class when they did so.) They came to class unprepared. They quoted the rules to him when he corrected them. They just didn't take him or his class very seriously. That's the problem, he concludes. Somehow I've given my students the message I don't have to be taken seriously. What do I do now?

*   *   *

It's a Friday afternoon in late September at Urbana Public Middle School. Mr. R., a first year teacher, is teaching a lesson to his eighth grade Principles of Democracy class.

"Devon Turner, read today's objective for us, please," Mr. R. instructs politely yet firmly looking directly at Devon Turner as he does so.

Devon reads the objective and the class is underway. As the students complete a short warm-up exercise, Mr. R. takes attendance and collects the previous night's homework. After a review of the warm-up, he instructs his students to prepare for a class forum. They arrange their desks in a large circle facing one another. Mr. R. has seated the students so those with weaker skills sit beside those with stronger skills *and talkative students beside quiet students. He reminds them of the procedures for class forums and then introduces the discussion. With few exceptions all goes well during the class, and as it concludes, Mr. R. feels a growing sense of pride. He has worked very hard to prepare for his first classes, and seeing his students learn in an organized and secure environment from the lessons he has planned for them gives him a wonderful feeling of accomplishment. He can't wait to teach his next class.*

The Control Conundrum

Since a class of thirty talkative, giggly, rambunctious elementary school students or thirty cynical, hormone-bathed, peer-pressured high school students can easily overwhelm anyone, managing student behavior is an important concern of all teachers. Because it is nearly impossible for effective learning to take place in chaos, you must control student dynamics and behavior in order for education to take place in your classroom.

Although a teacher must manage student behavior in order to teach, behavior management, in and of itself, is not teaching but merely crowd control. The teacher with the quietest classroom and most compliant students is not necessarily an effective teacher. Teaching requires imparting knowledge by encouraging curiosity and developing skills for independent learning. As a result, classrooms where good teaching is taking place will be noisy and seemingly disorganized at times.

Since this is your first class, you are probably very concerned about how to manage student behavior. Some veteran teachers will tell you to be really strict the first month of school while others will say to be benevolent and kind. What can you do to control your students so you can actually teach and enjoy it?

Prevent Problems Before They Start

Dealing with behavior problems not only wastes valuable teaching time but also produces a high degree of stress for everyone involved. The smart teacher uses planning and ingenuity whenever possible to avoid discipline problems.

Teach Lessons Suitable for Your Class

Activities suggested by texts, curriculum guides, or fellow teachers are not always appropriate for every class. You must be the ultimate decision-maker about the kinds of activities best suited for your class because you understand best the unique interpersonal dynamics, learning styles, and personal likes and dislikes that affect the teaching and learning taking place in your classroom.

As a beginner, however, you don't have a lot of experience on which to base these decisions and must at times rely on the suggestions of others. Unfortunately, a suggested lesson that worked very well with one teacher's class may wreak havoc with yours.

The eighth grade science text said I should have my class design and test fly their own paper airplanes as a motivational activity for a lesson on aerodynamics. It motivated them all right. It motivated them to behave like two-year-olds!

When I introduced this activity, they acted insulted, saying such things as, "Oh, goodie, goodie, we get to make paper planes today. Maybe tomorrow we'll get to make paper dolls." During the time they were working on this "fun motivational activity" their behavior was atrocious. They yelled across the room to one another, threw paper clips, and made obscene gestures with their planes. When it came time for them to "test fly" their creations they were so out of control the assistant principal had to come into my room to restore order! What a mess! Whoever came up with that "paper plane gimmick" didn't know anything about eighth graders.

When a fellow teacher raves about that super successful creative writing lesson that required her tenth graders to remove one of their shoes, place it on their desk and write a description of it, and you think such a lesson is a "wonderful idea," stop and ask yourself, "Is this lesson appropriate for the age, learning styles, grade level, interest level, and maturity level of my students?" If the answer to any of these is "no," think about modifying the lesson so that it better fits the nature of your class before attempting to teach it.

The activities and materials a teacher selects can have a positive or negative influence on the behavior of her class. In order for the influence to be positive she must be certain the work she assigns is appropriate for her unique group of students.

If your ninth grade class complains like crazy about the "smell" when Jamie Kelso, Earl Wilson, and Roberto Hernandez surreptitiously slip off their Reeboks during your second period English class, you know the "shoe lesson" as planned would generate lots of excitement but have limited educational value with this class. Knowing this, you can modify the lesson by perhaps having those students write a description of some less odoriferous object (for example, a backpack or a hat). Or, if your professional judgment tells you that any object you can possibly substitute will provide too much stimulus, you might opt not to teach that particular lesson altogether. This doesn't mean that if you have a difficult class you can or should avoid teaching exciting and dynamic lessons. It means you must set goals and work deliberately to change your students' behavior so they eventually are able to deal more maturely with this type of lesson.

The students presented with the paper plane activity obviously thought it beneath their level of sophistication, and told their teacher so in both words and deeds. Had the teacher thought carefully about the appropriateness of the activity for this class ahead of time, he might well have predicted what was going to happen and either chosen another motivational activity or set up the paper plane activity so his students saw it as challenging instead of childish. For example, he might have had a preliminary discussion with his class about how automobile, aircraft, and ship design engineers make models of their design ideas just to test them out.

The activities and materials a teacher selects can have a positive or negative influence on the behavior of her class. In order for the influence to be positive she must be certain the work she assigns is appropriate for her unique group of students.

Have Realistic Behavioral Expectations

To manage student behaviors more easily and effectively, you must have behavioral expectations that are realistic for your students and accept only the best possible behavior from them commensurate with their age and learning styles.

A class of first grade students is developmentally incapable of sitting still and being perfectly quiet for an extended period of time, and it is unrealistic to have such behavioral expectations for them. To do so sets a standard that is impossible for them to meet and causes them to be constantly "misbehaving." On the other hand, a class of high school students is quite capable of such self-control, and it is realistic to expect them to sit still quietly.

If you have a class with several ADD/ADHD children, it is unrealistic to expect them to sit quietly and attentively through an hour-long lecture on the merits of granting China Most Favored Nation trade status. In contrast, if you teach an honors economics class to strong auditory learners, such expectations are quite realistic.

As a beginner, you may have difficulty setting realistic behavioral expectations, and therefore be sent to observe another teacher to gain some "pointers" on how to do a better job. The problem with observing another teacher is that the more experienced teacher has different behavioral expectations and a different group of children than you do. So when you return to your class filled with "I'm going to make my class behave like Mr. Sergeant's class" fervor, your students, after a half-hour adjustment period, become more unruly than ever.

As a new teacher, you may find yourself frustrated because your class does not respond like another teacher's class, but you need to be aware that the dynamics in her class differ from those in yours. You cannot afford, however, to dismiss behavior management advice or training offered to you by more experienced teachers and mentors. To learn quickly, seek out and accept advice but tailor that advice to fit the needs of your class. Also, don't blame poor student behavior on the unworkable suggestions of others or the composition of the class. As a professional, it is your job to develop the judgment necessary to make correct educational decisions for your students and implement them effectively.

Develop Routine Procedures that Promote Acceptable Behavior

On the first day of school inform your students of the routine procedures they are expected to follow throughout the year. Then, during the first week, patiently remind them of your expectations and hold them gently accountable for meeting them.

You might, for example, expect your middle school students to enter the classroom quietly and on time, have the necessary materials with them, take their assigned seats, place their completed homework from the night before on their desks, and begin working on the warm-up activity that is written on the chalkboard.

You must have a clear idea of the procedures you want your class to follow and sound educational reasons for requiring them to do so. For example, students must:

- Enter the room quietly since they are transitioning from hallway behavior to classroom behavior.

Advice

Class routines, when fashioned, implemented, and reinforced with care, can quickly become habits that reduce behavior problems, increase the time spent on tasks, and promote a positive and stress-free learning environment. A routine procedure can be established for any frequently repeated class activity, for example:

- *Checking for homework completion.*
- *Distributing and collecting materials.*
- *Entering and leaving class.*
- *Asking to use the restroom, get a drink, see the school nurse.*
- *Traveling through the halls.*

- Have all materials with them because they can't do the assigned learning activities without the necessary materials.
- Take assigned seats as carefully planned seating can increase learning and decrease disruptions.
- Put their homework on their desks so it can be checked for completion and quickly collected while they work on the warm-up activity.
- Complete a warm-up activity so they can make the mental transition from their last class to this one and settle down from their hall activity.

A large portion of behavior problems takes place during less structured and less organized activities.

When students are expected from the first day of school to follow routine procedures when they arrive in your class, the majority will do so every day thereafter, provided you demonstrate the importance of those procedures by insisting that they be followed.

As a beginning teacher, avoid spending a great deal of class time justifying your choice of procedures since doing so leaves the impression that you are defensive and insecure. You must, however, clearly understand the rationale for your choice of procedures so that you are confident that your expectations are reasonable and necessary.

Determine Your Class Routines

Determining your class routines is another decision you must make based on the needs of your students and your teaching style. If your fourth grade students cannot hand in completed work without jumping out of their chairs, yelling out, "Wait, wait, you forgot my paper!" or refusing to stop working when they are reminded to do so several times, you definitely need to establish a "paper collecting" routine. When your tenth grade students stampede for the classroom door every time the bell rings, you definitely need to establish a dismissal routine.

Established habits are very difficult to overcome so use your student research and past interning or student teaching experience to infer where problems might occur and design routine class procedures to prevent them. As you do this, keep in mind that a large portion of behavior problems take place during less structured and less organized activities. The less organized an activity, the more likely inappropriate behavior will occur. Therefore, try to devise procedures that provide organization and structure appropriate to the maturity level of your class.

If you are assigned a group of fourth grade students with a reputation for rambunctiousness, and want to assure that they end the day in an orderly fashion, consider dismissing them individually based on whether they have completed all the steps required for dismissal, for example, picked up the area around their desk, put away all materials, put on their desk all books needed for that night's homework, and so on.

Establish Clear and Enforceable Rules

Students must have a clear understanding that you will not tolerate behaviors that interfere with the educational process. You can achieve this by establishing, explaining, and enforcing the class rules (euphemistically called behavioral guidelines, behavioral standards, or, in some cases, simply class procedures). It is your job, then, to create and enforce the requisite rules.

Few teachers relish the image of themselves as "the enforcer," but if you fail to enforce rules or establish unenforceable rules, you will create disciplinary problems and undermine your own authority.

Initially, the creating part seems deceptively easy. Simply draft rules that prohibit unacceptable behavior in your classroom. Problems arise, however, when those rules must be enforced. Few teachers relish the image of themselves as "the enforcer," but if you fail to enforce rules or establish unenforceable rules, you will create disciplinary problems and undermine your own authority. To prevent such occurrences, as you think of a class rule, ask yourself, "How am I going to enforce this rule? What are the consequences going to be if it is disregarded? Do I have the authority to

Make Realistic Rules

A rule that states, "Students may not talk among themselves unless given permission by the teacher to do so" is of better use than a rule that states, "Students in room 111 are always polite to one another." While the latter may be the ideal theoretical model, the former is the realistic educational practice. Although the latter is more positive in tone, it is so nebulous in scope that, when applied, it most certainly will require further explanation.

For example, if two students are having a "gab fest" while you are explaining the hypotenuse of a right triangle, it is more efficient and effective to remind them matter-of-factly of the "no talking among themselves rule" than it is to remind them of the "politeness to others" rule, which may then require a time-consuming explanation of politeness and rudeness.

carry out the consequences? Do I have the determination to enforce it consistently?" If you cannot answer these questions with some degree of certainty, you had better rethink the rule before finalizing it. (Be sure to read the information on enforcement and consequences discussed later before you do finalize your class rules.)

Another method of establishing rules is to have students write their own. This is usually not a viable strategy for the beginner, not necessarily because your students won't formulate acceptable rules (although it usually takes a skillful teacher to get them to do so), but because, as a first-year teacher, you need to project the image that you are in charge from day one. Students who write their own rules view themselves as empowered, as being on somewhat an equal footing with their teacher. While dealing with empowered students may not be a problem for a confident experienced teacher, it can be an enormous headache for the beginner who has not yet fully developed her own teaching style or the confidence that goes with it.

Consistently Reinforce Your Behavioral Expectations

At the beginning of the school year, it is best to stop instruction when you need to establish and reinforce your behavioral expectations. Model classes during the first weeks of school that turn into unruly mob scenes shortly thereafter frequently have teachers who rush to begin teaching at the expense of establishing and patiently reinforcing viable behavioral expectations. They often choose to ignore misbehavior in the hope that it will magically disappear and excuse their students' quickly deteriorating conduct with such explanations as, "This is just the wrong mix of kids! When the administrators put together this class, they put all the discipline problems in this group! I don't know what I'm supposed to do. These kids don't care about learning. They won't even give me a chance to teach them!" So if your class enters the room like a group of screaming banshees, you must not react like a banshee yourself. Instead, gain control by calmly and patiently demanding that they meet your expectations and hold them accountable for any unacceptable behavior.

Anticipate Problems to Prevent Them

The pragmatic teacher is an optimistic pessimist. Plan dynamic lessons that allow your students to discover and learn through hands-on activities and peer interaction. While you should expect the best from them, you should also understand your expectations will not always be met. To encourage the best behavior possible, anticipate potential problems and attempt to avoid them.

Anticipating problems is not all that difficult if you understand your students, pay close attention to the happenings in your school, and recognize when something is amiss.

If, for example, two students are arguing heatedly as they enter your room, do not thoughtlessly place them in the same work group later during the class, excuse them simultaneously to use the restroom, or call them into line one behind the other. Instead, after observing their angry behavior, try to prevent them from coming near each other. Also, calmly remind your class of the routine procedures they are expected to follow. Then, if necessary, quietly make arrangements for the irate students to speak with the school counselor individually.

Since you don't have a crystal ball, knowing what your students are going to do before they do it may seem impossible. Yet, anticipating problems is not all that difficult if you understand your students, pay close attention to the happenings in your school, and recognize when something is amiss.

You might know from observation and your student research that Marylee Thames (a student in your first period art class who intermittently spends weekends with her non-custodial parent) frequently arrives late for school on Mondays. When this happens, she doesn't have her school supplies, and is angry, confrontational, and disorganized.

Knowing this, you prepare for Monday by gently reminding Marylee on Friday afternoon to leave her school supplies for Monday in her locker. Should Marylee arrive late and in a foul mood on Monday morning, you are prepared for the onslaught, can avoid viewing her behavior as a personal affront, can calmly remind her of the class routines and expectations, and can deal with her tardiness at a time when she is less volatile and more receptive.

By using your powers of observation, understanding of students, and good judgment you can anticipate and avoid many impending behavior problems. Additionally, as a beginner use these tips to help you manage that first class more easily:
- Know students by name.
- Move around as you teach.
- Grade and return student work promptly.
- Rely on strategic seating arrangements.
- Communicate frequently with parents.
- Use calming activities when necessary.
- Plan extra carefully for "special activities".

Know Students By Name

Fewer sounds have the magical power to gain a person's attention than the sound of his own name. Often just calling students' names and then giving an instruction stops mischief before it becomes serious misbehavior. For example, "Kenishia, Marvin, and Adam, take your seats please and begin working on the warm up exercise." When managing behavior throughout your school (halls, cafeteria, lavatories, and such), the more students you know by name, the fewer disciplinary problems you're likely to have.

Your students won't expect you to know them by name on the first few days of school, but they will be impressed if you do. Conversely, they will have little regard for you if you don't care enough about them to learn their names. So, to earn the respect of your students and avoid creating negative attitudes, learn their names as quickly as your class size and schedule allows. Then, whenever opportunities arise, learn the names of even more students at your school.

Move Around as You Teach

To ensure your students' attention and deter their misbehavior, move around the classroom as you teach. By doing so you can not only better observe who is and who is not paying attention, but also provide extra support to those students who might need it.

Often by standing next to a "problem child," you can help him to settle down and focus. At times, just being in the right place at the right time can prevent a student-to-student confrontation that disrupts a lesson.

Grade and Return Student Work Promptly

One of the surest ways to keep students from misbehaving is to keep them focused on the work at hand. Hold them accountable for the quality of their work on a daily basis. It is your job to review student work thoroughly, grade it conscientiously, and return it promptly. If you procrastinate in grading and returning student work or don't bother to grade or return the work at all, you send the message that you don't really know or care whether your students are learning or not. Timely grading and returning of student work is not only essential to satisfactory behavior management but also to success as a teacher.

Rely on Strategic Seating Arrangements

The information provided in Chapter 3 suggests seating arrangements to avoid (or at least decrease) those pesky student behaviors that hinder the daily learning process in your classroom. Some additional seating arrangements may also prove helpful in keeping serious behavior problems from escalating into classroom crises:

- Seat the constantly angry, verbally abusive, anti-authority student, who in the past has refused to leave the classroom when directed to do so, near a classroom door. When you recognize the signs that this student is about to have problems, you can discreetly position yourself so she is cordoned between you and the classroom door and finds it easier and wiser to leave the room. (Do not, however, come in contact with the student or risk a physical confrontation. A low-keyed, even-tempered, well-designed, preemptive approach is always less stressful and more successful than an in-your-face, spur of the moment, overreaction.)
- Seat the fidgety hyperactive student on the periphery of the room, preferably at the back. This does not punish the student, but allows him the freedom to move about (for example, kneel on his chair, stand at his desk, or doodle in his notebook) without distracting others.
- Seat the insecure student who needs constant reassurance close to you at the beginning of the school year with the goal of slowly moving this student toward the middle of the room as the year progresses.
- Seat the attention-seeker (AKA, the class clown) away from your favorite main teaching area to avoid continual competition for your class' attention.
- Seat the ADD student away from high traffic areas where there are fewer distractions, and she can focus and attend better. (See page 169 for an example of a Strategic Seating Arrangement Chart.)

Communicate Frequently with Parents

Because their support is instrumental to their child's success in school and, therefore, your success as a teacher, work hard at developing a positive working relationship with the parents of your students. Keep them informed about their child's educational program and progress and avoid contacting them only when there are serious problems. (See Chapter 8 for more information on this topic.)

Use Calming Activities When Necessary

At times student behavior dictates that you use "calming activities" to rein in the class. Such behavior usually occurs when the school atmosphere is emotionally charged and student spirits are running high, for example, before a holiday or vacation, after a pep rally or an especially stimulating assembly, or at report card time.

Calming activities reduce the number of interactions among students, direct student focus, have a pacifying effect, and permit you to restore some semblance of order and breathe a deep sigh of relief.

When calming activities are used, teacher-to-student and student-to-student interaction is extremely limited and, depending upon the activity assigned, only minimal teaching and learning actually take place. If, however, you have a particularly difficult class, do not become dependent on such activi-

Sound Advice

Activities to Calm Students

- *Written practice work—work that students can easily complete independently*
- *Note taking or outlining—if actual note taking is too difficult, copying notes from the board or a transparency will do*
- *Illustrating a previously read story*
- *Drawing (or for younger students coloring)*
- *Crossword puzzles or word finds relating to previously taught lessons*
- *Hidden picture searches*
- *Heads down (for younger groups with few independent study skills)*
- *Clearing desks and sitting silently (See page 170 for more ideas.)*

---

ties as your main teaching strategy. Doing so can result either in students completing reams of valueless busy work while relying on you to control their behavior or in escalating behavior problems as students realize the banality of the assigned tasks and demonstrate their frustration and boredom by challenging your authority and displaying even more rebellious behavior. Calming activities are a survival strategy, and as such should be used sparingly and only when absolutely necessary.

Plan Extra Carefully for "Special Activities"

As disillusioning as it may seem, special activities such as field trips, sports days, class parties, and even recess often require more planning than regular classroom activities. Since these events are more stimulating, provide less structure, and alter the usual class routines, they can, unless carefully planned, result in student misbehavior and even student injury.

Again, conscientious preparation is the way to keep a day of fun from turning into a day of misery. Just as when planning a regular lesson, you must think carefully about any problems the special day might cause and plan accordingly.

The "special activity" with the greatest potential for mishap is the field trip. Since field trips take everyone away from the structure, protection, and support provided by the school setting, you must plan for them meticulously.

The ultimate goal of an educational field trip is, of course, to provide students with learning experiences not available at school, but to do so successfully, you must know beforehand what your students are going to see, do, and learn while on the trip. You must then be certain they understand how this trip relates to the information they are learning in school, how they will be held accountable for their learning and behavior during the trip, and precisely what the trip procedures will be. (See page 172 for an example of a Field Trip Checklist.)

Special Days Require Extra Attention

When planning a special day for your students, ask yourself the following questions:

- *Are the special activities so stimulating that you need to include some control activities at intervals throughout the day to settle everyone down? If so, what type of control activities would be most helpful?*
- *What special materials do you need?*
- *What is the backup plan should the activity be postponed? For example, the guest speaker doesn't arrive, the weather is inclement, or the buses don't arrive.*
- *What will you do if the activity takes longer than planned, for example, the buses coming back from the trip get stuck in traffic but your students must be back at school in time for dismissal?*
- *What procedures will you follow if there is an emergency, for example, a student is lost or injured or a traffic accident occurs?*
- *How will you monitor student behavior?*
- *How will you handle discipline problems?*
- *What special rules and procedures must your students follow in order to participate in this activity?*

Special activities generate enthusiasm and stimulate learning. They are essential to good teaching. They do, however, require extra planning to ensure their success.

A field trip is not a day off for you during which you can "kick back," assign your students to the care of others, and let them run roughshod over shopkeepers, museum guides, librarians, tour guides, restaurant patrons, and the public in general. It is an opportunity for students to "learn how to learn" and, in some cases, how to behave appropriately away from the classroom. At its best a field trip can be a memorable learning experience for all involved; at its worst, a catastrophe. The outcome almost always depends on whether you have planned thoroughly or haphazardly.

Meet the Challenge; Gain the Reward

Preventing behavior problems through thorough planning and insightful class management can be a challenging yet rewarding task. When your students are working well together and learning because of your efforts, you will feel a sense of satisfaction that motivates you to work even harder. This motivation will serve you well when you are confronted by behavior problems that you cannot prevent.

Notes

Chapter 7

Maintaining Control: Confronting Unavoidable Behavior Problems

"Children today are tyrants. They contradict their parents, gobble their food, and tyrannize their teachers."

—Socrates (470 B.C.)

 **Chapter 7**

Case Study—Mrs. Perez Passes Her First Test

It is the first day of school at Barclay Middle School, and Mrs. Perez is greeting students at the door of her classroom and directing them to their assigned seats.

"Hello, my name is Mrs. Perez. I'll be your reading teacher for this year. And your name is?"

"Desmond Gardner," replies a very tall muscular young man with a scowl. The students around him giggle and wink at one another nervously.

Mrs. Perez knows from her student research that Desmond Gardner is an academically gifted child who is shy and small for his age. She also knows that she has a six foot ten inch tall student in her class who stars on the school basketball team whose name is Germaine King. "Welcome to my class, Desmond. For the time being, I'd like you to sit at the seat assigned to Germaine King, and I'd like to speak with you at the end of class, please."

The students around the tall young man begin to laugh. "Busted!" One of them whispers. "The new lady got Germaine good!"

Mrs. Perez breathes a sigh of relief. She has won a small victory for control of her classroom. She knows from speaking with the other teachers that this is the most difficult class on her schedule, and that she must not back down when challenged by them, but instead, earn their respect by confronting their unacceptable behavior with ingenuity, resolve, a sense of humor, and several backup plans.

Managing Unavoidable Discipline Problems

Regardless of how skillful you are at preventing discipline problems, at some point you will have to deal head-on with students who challenge your authority and break the rules. While it's relatively easy to draft rules and formulate class routines, enforcing them is another matter entirely. You must convince students that they have more to gain by following the rules than by breaking them and devise ways to encourage acceptable behavior and discourage unacceptable behavior. You must do this within the constraints of the classroom, the prescribed curricular goals, the expectations of parents, and the parameters of good teaching. This is a difficult task and there are no simple ways to accomplish it. There are, however, some suggestions you can follow that may make the task of dealing with unavoidable discipline problems somewhat easier.

Enforce Rules From Day One

During the first few days of school, many new teachers make the mistake of disregarding minor infractions in an effort to "win over" their students. This behavior often causes students to conclude that you are either too insecure to enforce the rules or don't consider them worthy of enforcement. Unfortunately, you then face an uphill mettle-testing battle to make your students understand otherwise.

To manage student behavior successfully, you don't have to be mean-spirited and harsh but calm, persistent, and consistent. You must be certain your students understand your behavioral expectations and feel compelled to meet them. When they do not do so, you must hold them accountable by employing, depending on the seriousness of their misbehavior, everything from gentle reprimands to stern consequences.

Do not ignore unacceptable behavior in the hope that it will go away. It won't. (Even when "ignoring" is used as a viable behavioral strategy for managing severe "attention-getting" behaviors, the severe behavior intensifies before it actually stops.) Deal directly with problems when they occur and are relatively minor; don't wait until they grow into overwhelming obstacles.

Make Use of Positive Peer Pressure

If you set high (yet attainable) standards and teach your classes with fairness and professionalism, you will find the majority of your students well-behaved and obedient. Since they are in the majority, the well-behaved students create strong peer pressure that influences their less well-behaved classmates to conduct themselves appropriately.

The playful child who enters the classroom joking and laughing raucously finds it difficult to continue when her classmates settle into the class routine and react as if her behavior is "so immature." As long as you have a nucleus of students who follow the rules and routines, you can rely on them to act as role models who will exhibit a degree of positive influence over the entire class.

Tame the Tendency to Talk Too Much

When you must reprimand your students, say what must be said in a calm and relatively dispassionate manner and curb the tendency to pull out your soapbox. Remember, the longer you lecture your students regarding unacceptable behavior, the greater the likelihood they will stop listening and worsen the situation by behaving disrespectfully.

Also, avoid reprimanding a class (or student) when you are very angry. Count to ten, twenty, or even thirty, calmly tell your students that their behavior is totally unacceptable and that consequences will be forthcoming. Then, as quickly as possible, settle them into their regular class routines. You can decide on the consequences for their poor behavior when you are not angry and overly emotional.

> *To manage student behavior successfully, you don't have to be mean-spirited and harsh but calm, persistent, and consistent.*

Delay Your Response When You Don't Know How to Respond

If a discipline problem arises and you have no idea how to deal with it, a delaying tactic works best. Confront the offending student directly but delay discussing consequences for the misbehavior until a later time. A comment such as, "George, that type of behavior is unacceptable in this classroom. Please see me at the end of class (after school, during lunch, or during recess)," lets the offender, as well as the rest of the class, know that you won't tolerate the behavior and affords you some time to mull over your options for dealing with it. If possible, tailor the comment to the behavioral personality of the student. If you know from experience that when you say to George, "That type of behavior is unacceptable in this classroom," he will most likely reply, "What? I didn't do nothing! What did I do? It was Latisha! I didn't do nothing!" ask George to step into the hall where you can make the same remarks more privately or speak to him quietly at his desk after the class has settled down and begun working.

Another delaying tactic is the "planned delay." Use this tactic when you know exactly what the consequences for the misbehavior will be but want to wait for a more appropriate time before disclosing them (for example, when the least amount of disruption will take place or the offending student will be more receptive).

Both of these tactics are useful because they let students know you are aware of, care about, and are dealing with what is happening in your classroom. They know that you are in control and expect them to be in control.

Create an Artificial Shortage of Something Students Want

If you have a group of eighth graders who would rather socialize than focus on the day's lesson, you must contrive some type of behavior management system to stop their counterproductive classroom behavior. One way to do this is to create an artificial shortage of the commodity your students seem to want most: time to socialize. Then use that commodity as a reward.

For example, establish a rule that students may not talk among themselves when you are teaching, but make it clear that if they achieve the learning goals for a lesson more quickly than planned, they will earn time to socialize at the end of class. Then ensure their cooperative behavior by making certain they gain at least a few minutes of socializing time at the end of the first few classes. (The trick here is to allow just enough time at the end of the class to reinforce the desired behavior during class but not enough to create bedlam.) Also be careful to set behavioral guidelines for the socialization time so it does not deteriorate into shouting across the room, standing around in groups that turn into "the dominant member rules the herd" shoving matches or other unacceptable classroom behavior.

Once most of the students feel they will be treated fairly and accept your behavior management system (the artificially created shortage system), you have some control over those few remaining students who might continue to interfere with the educational process.

In the scenario above, you have taken a behavior that is plentiful in your classroom yet interferes with learning, but have limited and legitimized it on your own terms. While your students could totally ignore this behavior management system and socialize throughout the class, it is highly unlikely that the majority will do so providing they feel you have the courage of your convictions and are determined that learning will take place in your classroom.

To the casual observer, creating an artificial shortage may not seem to be a very effective way to stop misbehavior, but, in practice, it can and does work.

For example, a fifth grade class comes in from recess (or back from physical education) hot, thirsty, and rowdy. They know that in your classroom only

Advice

Activities that students enjoy (not only for fun but for status and power) can be useful when creating an artificial shortage. Among these (depending upon the policies of your school) might be:

- *Washing the boards*
- *Delivering a message to another room*
- *Getting a drink of water*
- *Distributing or collecting papers*
- *Writing on the chalkboard*
- *Coloring or drawing*
- *Socializing*
- *Eating a snack*
- *Being line leader or ender*
- *Being first to lunch*
- *Being team captain*
- *Listening to music*
- *Sitting next to a friend*
- *Presenting a play*

students who are seated and working quietly can get drinks. The majority of students settle down and begins working. (They do this because this is the behavior that is consistently expected of them, and also, they know they will be allowed to get drinks if they do so.) You then permit students who are behaving appropriately to get drinks (one at a time or in very small groups). Students who ignore the class rules soon notice they are being left out of something everyone else is enjoying and either follow through or complain that they haven't had a chance to get their drink. If they follow through, you have nothing more to do. If they complain, you remind them of the rules, and when they follow through, permit them to get drinks also.

If you set high (yet attainable) standards and teach your class-es with fairness and professionalism, you will find the majority of your students well-behaved and obedient.

Determine the Truth About Consequences

Since most, if not all, behavior management systems use both positive and negative consequences, you will often be placed in the unenviable position of determining what those consequences will be. Creating artificial short-ages helps you create rewards and punishments that, depending upon when and how they are used, can be viewed by a student as positive or negative. At times, however, a student's behavior is so egregious that it demands more stringent consequences. You must then work within the dic-tates of your particular school system to arrive at appropriate punishments for serious offenders, and, in truth, your options are quite limited. (This is why it is better to prevent behavior problems through foresight and good planning and/or keep them minor by using the "artificial shortage tech-nique," than it is to deal with them when they become totally outrageous.) You can isolate a student from his peers, keep him from participating in a favorite activity, or request the assistance of others in dealing with him.

Use Isolation As Insulation

When a student is such a "live wire" that she keeps herself and everyone around her from learning, a fitting consequence is isolation from the group. You can accomplish this within the classroom by moving the "electric personality" to an area of the room where she cannot be seen by her peers nor interact with them (yet can still be monitored by you). Providing the classroom is large enough, you can create such an area by arranging furniture (such as bookcases or moveable chalkboards) to make an alcove to be used not only as an "isolation booth," but as a reading room, conference room, and individual instructional area.

If the classroom is too small for such an arrangement or the "electric child" still creates problems when isolated within the room, you may be able to work out an exchange isolation agreement with a neighboring teacher. You would send the child who needs to be isolated from her peer group to a neighboring classroom when absolutely necessary, and the neighboring teacher would do the same when faced with a similar problem. This type of exchange is possible only as long as the exchange student does not wreak havoc on the class to which she is sent. You must therefore send enough independent work with the student to keep her from disrupting the other classroom and must not impose on the receiving teacher by sending students to his room too frequently.

Since the child with the electric personality is often motivated by a strong desire for attention (be it positive or negative), as soon as she behaves appropriately you must reward the child by giving her attention. If you do not do so, she will eventually contrive ways to gain attention even when isolated.

Require Students to Forfeit a Favorite Activity
The consequence most used for flagrant rule breaking is to keep the student from participating in a favorite activity for a period of time. The forfeited activity might be recess, lunch time, before school time, after school time, an assembly, a field trip, or some other special activity such as a school dance or participation in a sport.

In most school systems, the use of detention to forfeit after school time is less common today than in the past because many students do not live within walking distance of their school. If they are detained, arrangements must be made for their transportation home. Also, forfeiture of lunch time does not mean denying students their nourishment, but depriving them of time to socialize with their peers.

Successful use of forfeitures requires forethought and good judgment. Clear communication must take place between you, the administration, and parents when a student is to be kept from an especially important favorite activity (for example, sports day, field trip, special performance) as a consequence of poor behavior. (See Chapter 8.) When a child has behaved appropriately for a majority of the forfeited time, consider permitting him to participate briefly in the forfeited activity before its conclusion. This not only tells him that he is back in your "good graces," but also allows him to "save face" with his classmates, and helps him return to class with a positive attitude.

A good rapport with students often is nurtured by a sensitive enforcement of consequences for their misbehavior.

You may be concerned that allowing a student to participate in a forfeited activity, even for a brief period of time, will undermine your disciplinary program. When done wisely, however, it helps insure cooperative behavior in the future.

A good rapport with students often is nurtured by a sensitive enforcement of consequences for their misbehavior. If the purpose of imposing a consequence is to change a child's behavior, you will quickly discern whose conduct improves when the consequences are stringent and whose deteriorates, and will apply this information judiciously in everyone's best interest. Whenever possible, refrain from stating beforehand precisely how stringent a consequence will be because once you make such a statement, you must follow through. For example, instead of saying "George, that's it! You've called out one too many times in my classroom! You now owe me your entire recess period!" you would say, "George, that's it! You've called out one too many times in my classroom! You now owe me some of your recess time!" (Exceptions to this policy of stating consequences explicitly would be strict behavior modification programs that permit you no latitude in implementation.)

Generally speaking, one of the worst mistakes you can make when imposing forfeits is to deprive a child of participation in a favorite activity for an exorbitant period of time. Protracted punishments (a week or a month) build only bitterness and resentment and are extremely difficult, if not impossible, to enforce.

Sometimes you may realize (after the fact) that a consequence is unsuitable for a specific child. If this happens, and it should not happen often if you have done your student research, admit that the consequence is unrealistic and quickly modify it.

For example, you might tell an ADHD third grader to sit quietly with his hands folded on his desk for fifteen minutes as a consequence for constantly calling out. After two or three tries it is obvious the child is unable, even by making his best effort, to sit still for longer than five minutes. You would then adjust your expectations to bring them more in line with the student's ability level since to do otherwise could easily turn a relatively minor behavior problem into a major behavioral ordeal.

> *One of the worst mistakes you can make when imposing forfeits is to deprive a child of participation in a favorite activity for an exorbitant period of time.*

Don't Overdo It

Children want and need the security of adult control and guidance in their lives, but it must be given with kindness and consideration. When it becomes necessary to use negative consequences, do only what you absolutely must to control counterproductive behavior. Browbeating students into total submission causes them to feel humiliated and resentful, not respected and cooperative.

Proceed cautiously when reprimanding a child for poor behavior and avoid correcting the child in front of the entire group. Speak firmly, but do not scream, shout, or resort to sarcasm since doing so runs the risk of causing students to respond in kind, and it's difficult for effective communication to take place where there is discordant noise and derisiveness.

Also, never punish the entire class for the misdeeds of a few. The unfairness of such a punishment usually creates such a high degree of student indignation that rebellion ensues. When, however, you are certain that the majority of your class (roughly eighty percent or more) has behaved disgracefully (for example, participated in a food fight in the cafeteria or sabotaged a substitute's class) begin by "dressing down" the entire group and then quickly excuse those few students who are innocent of wrongdoing from your entire "I am so embarrassed by the behavior of my class" lecture. This protects the innocent from being unfairly punished.

Request the Help of Others

If you have used preventive techniques, created artificial shortages, and devised and administered negative consequences, and a child's behavior is still unacceptable, it's time to request help from someone with more expertise and/or authority. This might be the child's parent, an administrator, or a student support person. Also, depending upon the procedures followed by your particular school district, you can request help from the school's Admissions, Review, and Dismissal Team (a group consisting of everyone previously mentioned that meets to determine how to help at-risk children).

Proceed cautiously when reprimanding a child
for poor behavior and avoid correcting the child
in front of the entire group.

Before you request help, however, be sure you have made every effort to deal with the child's behavior yourself, not because your ego is involved, but to build a positive rapport with your students. Often children feel that what happens between themselves and their teacher is confidential and not subject to teacher "tattling." While this doesn't mean you should avoid candid and tactful communication with administrators, parents, and support personnel, it does mean you must avoid constantly running to the office, calling parents, or seeking out support personnel to complain about a student's flagrant disregard of even minor rules.

As with all professional decisions, use good judgment when deciding to request help. Do not request help when you can handle a problem on your own, but be sure to do so before a problem becomes insurmountable or, even worse, dangerous.

> *Often children feel that what happens between themselves and their teacher is confidential and not subject to teacher "tattling."*

Help from Parents

When you must request the help of parents in dealing with their child, tactfully explain the problem, listen carefully to what they have to say (see Chapter 8 for more information on this subject), and be prepared to suggest what they could do to support you in working to improve their child's conduct.

Your part of the conversation might sound something like, "Mrs. Jones, regardless of what I do to keep Johnny from talking when he should be listening, I can't seem to get him to stop. I've isolated him from the group and taken away his recess time and these consequences have only worked for a day or two. I know that he wants very much to please you and do well in school and so was wondering if the next time he disturbs the class and is kept from recess, I might have him make a phone call or write a letter to you explaining his conduct in my class." If the parent suggests a different strategy for working with the child, you can use it instead of yours. Don't, however, expect parents to offer solutions for school-based problems, only support in dealing with them. Therefore, strategies such as having the child explain his unacceptable behavior to his parents are appropriate and effective when dealing with some types of student misconduct.

Help from Support Personnel

When requesting the help of support personnel, discuss not only the student's negative behaviors, but also the strategies you have employed in dealing with them, the effectiveness of those strategies, and any pertinent information regarding other issues that may be affecting the student (for example, a death in the family, a divorce, or a parent's illness or job loss). Bear in mind that each support person has his or her own particular professional stance when dealing with student problems. The counselor will suggest strategies that incorporate a counseling approach, the school psychologist a psychological approach, and the school nurse a health care approach, and so on. Therefore, if you feel strongly that a support person's specific professional approach is not best for the problem you are attempting to solve, you should not waste that person's time seeking advice you do not intend to use.

Help from Administrators

When all else fails, there's always the office. But again, unless the misbehavior is sudden and serious, referring a student to the office also requires proper preparation. If you are having persistent problems with a child and

Sound Advice

The Teacher as Authority Figure

*It is fashionable today to downplay the role of the teacher as authority figure. In some school systems the title "teacher" has been replaced by the euphemism "facilitator," as a way of demonstrating to students that they are on an equal footing with their teacher. The fallacy of this type of thinking becomes apparent when as the teacher you must make decisions concerning the education of your students and be held accountable for the results caused by your decisions. Regardless of the egalitarianism of a prevailing educational philosophy, **you** are the one held responsible when students fail to make progress academically, and so must always retain a certain amount of power and authority to meet that responsibility. A teacher can easily relinquish authority but not responsibility.*

are in constant contact with the parent, you should inform an administrator about what is happening. She can then not only provide you with the support of her authority when dealing with the child but also suggest strategies you might try when doing so. It's a good idea to request in writing (see Chapter 9) a meeting with the appropriate administrator to discuss your concerns about the "problem child." At this meeting, describe the child's unacceptable behavior, the intervention strategies you have tried, and any future strategies you want to employ that need an administrator's support (such as office detention or suspension from school). Take notes and restate in your own words the agreed-upon strategy. If, for instance, you understand your administrator to agree that the student is to be sent to the office the next time she gives you a hard time, your restatement might be, "Then we agree that the office will deal with Tiffany Mays the next time she is blatantly disrespectful to me."

Chapter 8

Communicating: Conveying the Right Message

"Too often we underestimate the power of a touch, a smile, a kind word, a listening ear, an honest compliment, or the smallest act of caring, all of which have the potential to turn a life around."

—Leo Buscaglia

Inside Chapter 8

Case Study—Mr. Chadwick's Speech Blunder

It's a Tuesday morning at Morning Side Elementary School. Mr. Chadwick has arrived a little later than usual because he overslept. Monday evening was Parent Conference Night, and he was late getting home. He is tired, and he's hoping for a peaceful day. As he approaches his classroom, he finds Mrs. Lawson, the speech/language pathologist standing outside his classroom door.

"Morning, Mrs. Lawson. You waiting for me?"

"Good morning, Mr. Chadwick. I need to speak with you about something important."

"Sure, come inside."

"Mr. Chadwick, I believe you had a conference with Lamar Parsons' parents last night?"

"Yes, I did. It went very well, too. They are pleased with the progress he's making but have some concerns about his speech . . ."

"I'm aware of their concerns," interrupts Mrs. Lawson. "What exactly did you say to the Parsons about Lamar's speech problem?"

"Well, I told them that we have an excellent Speech/Language Pathologist here at Morning Side, and if they felt Lamar needed help with his articulation, I would make arrangements for you to give him speech therapy."

"That's not the way it's done, Mr. Chadwick!" states Mrs. Lawson her voice calm but her demeanor angry. "You had no business telling the Parsons I would provide speech therapy for Lamar. First, Lamar has had a thorough speech/language evaluation, and he has no significant articulation problems. You would have known this if you had reviewed his records BEFORE you made my commitments for me! Second, there is a procedure teachers MUST follow to get support services for their students. The first step in that procedure is to speak with the support person or fill out a referral. Did you speak with me? Did you fill out a referral?"

"Well, I just thought that it's the speech person's job to help kids with speech problems so I told the parents to see you."

"No, Mr. Chadwick, that's not what you did! You didn't just tell them to see me. If

that's what you had said, I wouldn't be so upset with you. You told them I would pro-vide speech therapy for Lamar! I can't do that because Lamar doesn't need therapy!"

"I guess I didn't realize what I was actually saying. I'm sorry, Mrs. Lawson."

"I'm afraid sorry won't do, Mr. Chadwick. You see, the Parsons have demanded that Lamar be given speech therapy, and every other support service the school provides, for the past three years. Every year he's given a thorough evaluation, and every year that evaluation shows he doesn't need services. Last night the Parsons came beating on my door telling me that Mr. Chadwick said I must give their son individual speech therapy. Now Mr. Chadwick, since you created this mess, it's your job to straighten it out."

Communication is Everything

Since effective communication is the essence of good teaching, you must be able to communicate clearly, accurately, and tactfully. Not only must you explain curricular concepts and behavioral standards so that students of varying aptitudes can understand and attain them, but you must be able to convey information about students' abilities, skill levels, behaviors, and progress diplomatically to parents, administrators, support personnel, and fellow staff members. Also, since indirect communication often has an even greater impact than direct communication, you must be certain that your actions agree with your words.

Communicating with Parents

It is never too early to open the lines of communication with parents. In almost every instance, the sooner you gain respect and support from par-ents, the sooner you gain respect and cooperation from children. This is why an introductory call home (see Chapter 1) is so important, and why it's a good idea to have positive communication with parents before cir-cumstances force you to have negative communication with them. If the parents of a difficult-to-manage child are contacted only when he misbe-haves, they soon come to the conclusion that you don't like their child and are unfairly impugning him.

The Parent-Teacher Conference

As with all aspects of teaching, the key to success when communicating with parents is careful preparation. To prepare properly for a parent-teacher conference, first have a clear understanding of its purpose. Is it to present an overall progress report or to discuss a specific concern about behavior, curriculum, peer dynamics, attendance, homework, or adjustment to school? If a parent requests a conference and you are not sure why, politely ask. Once you know the purpose, you can prepare accordingly.

General meetings such as "Back to School Night" usually require you to present an overview of such topics as the school year's curriculum, your behavioral and academic expectations, and information specific to your school and school district. Many schools also schedule semi-annual or quarterly conferences so teachers can discuss student progress with parents.

Meetings to discuss a specific concern, such as lack of academic progress or unacceptable behavior, require you to compile and review standardized test scores, anecdotal records, referrals to support personnel or the office, notes home, work samples, and records of strategies employed to help the child. Such preparation not only helps show the efforts you have made to help the child, but also bolsters your confidence when you meet with parents.

Here are some guidelines you can follow to assure productive parent-teacher conferences:

- Begin positively.
- Communicate in terms that everyone can understand.
- Discuss only the child in question.
- Avoid promises you can't keep.
- Share negative information tactfully.
- Offer suggestions for dealing with problems.
- Strive for a happy ending.

Begin Positively

Begin the parent-teacher conference on a positive note. Report on the progress the child has made in academic and social areas and mention his positive attributes. If you feel unusually nervous about a particular meeting, write yourself a few reminder notes to help you start off on the right foot. You might jot down, for example, Belinda Marshall: reading on grade level, actively participates in class discussions, helpful and kind to others, well organized, plays junior varsity softball.

Communicate in Terms that Everyone Can Understand

To sound authoritative and professional teachers sometimes use terminology that even their fellow educators can't understand without referring " to the current literature" or the latest "educational acronyms reference guide." Since the purpose of a parent conference is to communicate, not to confuse, avoid educational jargon and pretentious language.

If you tell parents that you "antiseptically bounced" their child because she was "verbally opprobrious" (instead of telling them their daughter was sent out of the room to cool off because she was speaking disrespectfully), you are not conveying superior meaning but superior attitude. Always attempt (without resorting to speech that is profane or undignified) to use language parents understand. If you must use specialized terminology, stop and explain its meaning in lay terms.

Discuss Only the Child in Question

Sometimes parents will want to discuss the progress or behavior of other children in the class. It is at best unprofessional and at worst a serious breach of confidentiality for you to engage in this type of conversation. If a parent encourages you to do so, refuse to comment or comment only generally, and then direct the conference back to their child. For example, if a parent says, "Little Jimmy tells me that Bronwin Miller is always disrupting the class. I certainly hope you are going to inform her mother." Your reply might be, "All children have their difficult moments, but overall everyone is making satisfactory progress . . . Do you have any other questions regarding Jimmy's progress?"

Avoid Promises You Can't Keep

When conferencing with parents beware of promising them more than you can deliver and never ever promise the services of other professionals without their prior approval and, more wisely, their participation in the conference. When parents inquire about additional services (such as reading, counseling, or tutoring) explain that you will discuss their request with the proper support persons and be back in touch with them as quickly as possible. Then be sure to follow through!

Share Negative Information Tactfully

If you schedule a conference with the goal of informing parents that their child is always angry and often has trouble controlling his temper, you must present such information tactfully. First, as mentioned earlier, be sure to share some positive information about the child, and then ask questions to determine if he is having the same problems outside of school. (For example, How is Johnny is doing at home? What does he do for fun after school? Does he get along okay with children in the neighborhood?)

The parents' responses may indicate that Johnny is having behavioral problems at home as well as at school. His mother might say that he likes to play outdoor sports with the kids in the neighborhood, but he's so competitive that he frequently gets into fights with them.

If you are fortunate enough to have the parent express your concerns in their words, you know they are, at least to some degree, aware of Johnny's problems and, quite possibly, will view your concerns as valid.

If the parents articulate their awareness of the problem, you can gently and unemotionally explain that you are having some of the same problems with Johnny at school. Then, carefully delineate them using the documentation you have prepared prior to the conference, and request their support to help overcome them.

Conversely, if the parents tell you that Johnny is well behaved, has lots of friends, and seldom gets angry when at home, you must tactfully report your observations regarding his opposite behavior at school. You might say for example, "I'm so glad he's doing well at home, but unfortunately he sometimes has a hard time controlling his temper here at school. For instance, yesterday he got very upset with the child seated next to him because she said she didn't have a pencil to lend him. He then got a mouthful of water from the fountain, and spit it in the girl's face. When I told him his behavior was unacceptable, and asked him to apologize to the child, he kicked over his desk and ran out of the room screaming, "I'm not going to apologize and you can't make me!"

Take care not to overstate your case since doing so can easily turn parents' helpful supportiveness into detrimental defensiveness. Avoid recounting in great detail and accusatory tones all of the child's past misdeeds even though you are well prepared to do so. The purpose of the conference is to inform the parents about their child's behavior and gain their support in dealing with it, not to vent your frustrations.

Offer Suggestions for Dealing with Problems

Once you have tactfully stated your concern, ask the parents if they have any suggestions for dealing with the child's behavior. If they do, listen carefully and agree to try those that seem most workable. If they don't, offer some of your own. For example, you might agree to send a note or behavior checklist home daily or arrange for everyone to meet with the school counselor or you might request that a parent come to school and observe the child's behavior in the classroom.

Strive for a Happy Ending

A positive ending to a parent-teacher conference is as important as a positive beginning. Conclude with a brief review of the topics you have covered, a recap of any suggested solutions to problems, and a positive statement about the child. Habitually end a conference by thanking parents for their attendance, concern, and continued support.

Dealing with Angry Parents

The best advice about meeting with angry parents is, if at all possible, don't. When you must communicate unpleasant news to parents, prepare them with a prompt preliminary phone call followed by a formal conference scheduled a day or two later, thus affording the parents a cooling off period. Therefore, when Brandon ties Libin's shoelaces together during art class and Libin falls face forward into the green tempera paint, call Libin's parents before the resplendently green Libin arrives home. While this action won't necessarily prevent Libin's parents from being furious, it will prepare them to greet their jaded son sympathetically and also convey the message that you deal with discipline problems quickly and forthrightly.

> *Observations instead of explanations depersonalize the discussion by adding objectivity and communicate that you are not biased and defensive but open and reasonable.*

If an angry parent confronts you, remain calm and behave professionally. Try to play the role of a reasonable, even-tempered schoolteacher. Don't take what is said personally, but, at the same time, don't subject yourself to unwarranted abuse. If, in your judgment, the parent seems totally out of control, excuse yourself, leave the area, and seek the assistance of an administrator. Otherwise, allow the parent to vent his frustration, listen carefully to what he says, and after he concludes, as a means of clarification, restate his concerns in your words. Next, gently present your observations regarding the incident. Observations instead of explanations depersonalize the discussion by adding objectivity and communicate that you are not biased and defensive but open and reasonable.

For example, you are confronted after school by a parent demanding to know why you made his child miss the school bus. He is furious because he had to leave work to pick up the child and angrily tells you so. Although you may feel somewhat intimidated by his ire, you remain calm and attempt to see things from his perspective. He's in a conference at work, his eleven year old daughter, upset and crying, calls him on her cell phone and says, "Daddy, the teacher didn't dismiss us on time, and I missed my bus! All the buses are gone! How am I going to get home?"

You calmly tell the father that you understand why he is upset, that you are sorry that his daughter missed her bus and he had to leave an important work conference to pick her up. You do not shout back (or explain tearfully) in your defense that the child was dismissed on time along with everyone else in the class and none of the other children missed their buses.

After he has had time to vent his frustration and is more receptive to what you have to say, explain equably your observations regarding the class dismissal. (Students were called to their buses at 3:30, all the students in your class were dismissed from your room immediately, no one was held back, no one was in the hall outside of your room after dismissal.)

Communicating with Administrators

The golden rule for communicating with administrators is "make sure you do." Those responsible for the safety and education of all of the students in your school take a dim view of learning about parent problems, student difficulties, or, worse yet, a growing crisis at the last moment. It is your job as a professional to communicate essential information to your administrators.

Determine the Essential Information

In theory an administrator's top priority is quality of instruction, but in practice public relations and safety issues almost always take greater precedence. Your administrator doesn't want to know in minute detail how hard you've worked to get your fifth period English class to stop splitting their infinitives, but he does want to know (in order to be prepared for the forthcoming parental onslaught) that Ariel Cooper, whose parents are vocal and persistent critics of school policies, is in danger of failing English.

Above all you must inform the appropriate administrator of any behavior that compromises student safety. If, for example, you discover that Patrick Lang, a student in your first period algebra class, has brought a box cutter to school, no matter how nice a kid Patrick may be, how sure you are that he just forgot it was in his coat pocket from work last night, and how determined you are to keep this kid in school, you must, as a professional, report the incident to an administrator. (See Chapter 9 for suggestions on the best ways to do this.) If you fail to follow through and Patrick seriously injures someone, both you and your administrator will be held accountable for not assuring the safety of the students in your class and school respectively.

If you are extremely lucky and no one is injured by Patrick and his box cutter, but students, parents or, worse still, the media learn that he was not held accountable for a serious rule infraction, your administrator won't be the only educator required to offer an explanation to the local school board. Also, by not informing the administration of Patrick's box cutter, you are sending the message to Patrick (and any other students who are aware of this incident) that you do not support your school's discipline policy or those who enforce it. When this happens, troublesome students view you as their comrade-in-arms instead of as their teacher, and your ability to control your class can be quickly compromised.

> *The golden rule for communicating with administrators*
> *is "make sure you do."*

Communicate Your Concerns to Administrators Effectively

You can take a few basic steps to communicate significant concerns to administrators effectively:

- Schedule an appointment.
- Prepare carefully.
- Take notes.
- Review recommendations.
- Avoid criticizing your fellow teachers.

Schedule an Appointment

Because of the many demands placed on administrators' time and attention, communicating effectively with them requires a slightly different approach than communicating with others. If you want to speak with them about specific issues such as on-going problems with student discipline, the best methods to implement curriculum guidelines, or suggestions for inservice courses that might be most useful to you, request an appointment. Do this even if your administrator is a very approachable easy-going person who prides herself on her "open-door" policy. Requesting an appointment assures you of a block of time to meet with your administrator, discuss your concerns, and gain her advice and support.

Be Prepared (Again)

To ensure that all of your concerns are covered during the allotted time, you must prepare accordingly. Jot down the topics you want to discuss and collect any documentation germane to your concerns (such as student work samples, parent notes, or lesson plans). During the meeting, state your concerns professionally and provide any documentation you have to support them. It's acceptable at this time to trot out some of that pedagogical terminology you learned in college. If you believe that Matt Janczewski, the star quarterback on your high school's football team, cheated on his trigonometry midterm, you must not be surprised or offended when asked for proof. Also be prepared for the possibility that your administrator may offer solutions that you find unacceptable. Should this happen, tactfully explain why you believe the suggested solution is impractical. Keep in mind that when you seek assistance from an administrator, the advice rendered is offered with the expectation that it will be taken. So, ask for an administrator's advice only when you are prepared to follow it.

Take Notes and Review Any Recommendations

Take notes during an administrative meeting, and conclude it by summarizing the recommended courses of action. Such a summary helps prevent misunderstandings about what is to be done and who is to do it. When summarizing the meeting about the cheating quarterback you might say, "My main reason for requesting this meeting, Ms. Smith, was to inform you that I believe Matt Janczewski cheated on his midterm and to ask your advice about dealing with his dishonesty. You think that because the proof I have of Matt's cheating is largely circumstantial, I should give him another midterm. You will contact Matt's parents regarding this incident and I will make a follow-up call later this week."

When you seek assistance from an administrator, the advice
rendered is offered with the expectation that it will be taken.

Avoid Criticizing Fellow Professionals

Unless serious safety issues are involved, do not discuss other teachers' weaknesses with your administrators, but when given the opportunity, do genuinely praise their strengths. Should you have a serious concern about the behavior of a fellow teacher, as a mature professional you must communicate that concern to him directly and tactfully.

Communicating with Staff Members

If you are entering the teaching profession directly from college and your previous work experience has been in jobs working with others in your age group, you may find communicating in a school setting somewhat different. Your comrades-in-teaching will range in age from your peers to, in some cases, your grandparents' peers. In order to be understood and respected, communicate in standard English and eschew the use of slang expressions and four-letter expletives.

No matter how great the temptation, avoid criticizing other teachers behind their backs. Also, until you gain more teaching experience, criticizing them to their faces isn't such a wonderful idea either. Sometimes as "the new kid on the block" you can be manipulated by a seemingly kind fellow educator with her own agenda into a discussion of another teacher's failings. Such statements frequently find their way back to the one being criticized and can then prove harmful to your standing in the school community. They can also prove detrimental to your career several years later when the maligned teacher is promoted to supervisor and still recalls in vivid detail exactly what you said about him.

Communicating in Writing

Written communication, whether it is for students, parents, administrators, or fellow staff members, requires special attention to detail. Careless spelling, grammar, punctuation, usage, as well as poorly expressed ideas can leave the impression that you are either apathetic or poorly educated, neither of which is helpful to your image as a competent teacher. Also, take care to use only behavioral observations when writing reports about your students and to be precise in your descriptions. (See Chapter 9 for more information on this topic.)

Communicating Through Actions

The old expression "actions speak louder than words" is most important to teachers. Students are always observing their teachers' behavior and noticing any discrepancies between what they say and what they do. Every inconsistency and failure to follow through can breed mistrust and even contempt for those in authority. Your role is to teach children to think for themselves and question blatant misuse of authority, not to demonstrate through careless and/or self-indulgent behavior that authority figures are inherently duplicitous. So, if students are not to talk to one another during a guest's speech because it is rude for them to do so, then you also may not have a conversation with a fellow teacher during the speech. If students may not chew gum in your classroom, you may not chew gum either. If students must hand in their term papers on time, you must grade and return them on time. Your belief in the standards set for your students is communicated to them through your behavior. Therefore, your actions must always agree with your words.

Chapter 9

Documenting: Having the Write Stuff

*"A memorandum is written not to inform
the reader but to protect the writer."*

—Dean Acheson

Inside Chapter 9

Case Study—Ms. Marksley Takes Note

Ms. Marksley is in the middle of a science lesson on gravity when the office secretary enters her room and hands her a note.

"Ms. Marksley,
We have an emergency and must know when, during the past month, Tommy Steck was absent from your first period science class. Also, we must see any notes his parents sent to you regarding those absences as well as Tommy's work portfolio. M.A.G."

Ms. Marksley looks at the waiting secretary in confusion. "Does this mean they want this material right this minute?" she asks quietly. "Can't it wait until the end of this class?"

The secretary gives her a sympathetic look and shakes her head no.

Ms. Marksley directs her students to review chapter 9 in their textbooks and sets out to collect the requested documentation. Fortunately, she keeps up-to-date records and well-organized files. After a few minutes of searching, she gives the secretary the necessary material and returns to teaching her class.

Good Record Keeping Equals Good Teaching

An integral part of a teacher's job is recordkeeping. As strange as it may seem, thorough documentation can actually improve your teaching as well as your communication with parents, staff members, and administrators; your performance evaluations; and your ability to ward off lawsuits. Accurate and complete recordkeeping helps you better understand the dynamics taking place in your classroom. Good records keep you informed about your students. You know which students:

- Are making satisfactory or unsatisfactory progress
- Are working at, below, or above grade level
- Are completing independent work satisfactorily
- Participate in only certain types of lessons
- Like or dislike practice and review lessons
- Like or dislike discovery lessons
- Are completing homework

- Have mastered concepts
- Need more practice
- Are totally confused
- Have certain patterns of absence or lateness
- Have certain patterns of misbehavior
- Have cooperative or uncooperative parents

The Write Stuff to Keep

As a beginner, keep every document given to you (including e-mail) with the exception of advertising literature and duplicate announcements. Keep copies of anything you write to or for others. Correspondence with parents, student work samples, records of important daily events, notes and reports sent to administrators and supervisors, as well as reminders sent to other staff members can prove helpful throughout the school year.

Correspondence with Parents

When a parent sends a note, be sure it is dated and then put it in a "notes received" envelope. When you send a note to a parent, keep the original in a "notes sent" envelope and, if possible, send a photocopy home. If you don't have access to a copier or lack the time to make copies, record in a "notes sent" log the purpose of the note and the date it was sent. Also save e-mail correspondence and back it up or print it.

Samples of Student Work

Save samples of graded and returned student work. Keep these in individual portfolios stored in an easily accessible area of the classroom. (Keeping them in students' desks is not a good idea since, even with careful pruning, they become unwieldy and bushy.)

Portfolios that include a genuine sampling of student work (the good, the bad, the ugly) provide excellent documentation of student progress. When, however, a child is making little to no progress, it's best to keep most of the unsatisfactory papers in your own separate file. To build student confidence and promote positive public relations, some schools require teachers to keep a "showcase portfolio" of each student's best work. If your school has such a policy, keep a "showcase" but also a "reality case."

Prompt and thorough grading and return of student work serves notice to students that they are accountable for the quality of their work. When graded papers are retained in a portfolio, students are motivated to focus on the comments and grades given their work, ask questions about them, and learn from the written feedback.

Although the whole process of portfolio management may sound cumbersome and time-consuming, if carefully planned and implemented, it actually takes a minimum amount of time and is worth the extra effort. You can set aside about a half-hour once a week (less for middle and high school students who, because they see the teacher for only one subject, have fewer papers to review and organize), for students to place, organize, and review the papers in their portfolio. This review process gives students an excellent opportunity for self-evaluation and, many times, causes even seemingly indifferent students to question their progress or lack thereof.

Advice

Put it in Writing

A file (or log) of notes to and from parents:

- *Provides a record of notes received from parents. If a parent is angry because you did not respond promptly to a mysteriously missing missive, you can use your bulging "notes received envelope" to verify you did not receive the note and show that you do chronicle parents' correspondence.*
- *Documents the efforts made by you and the parents to resolve problems.*
- *Reveals behavioral patterns. (For example, a note about problems with math homework every Monday night, even when easy review assignments are given, indicates the problem is not about math homework.)*
- *Provides essential information if you are asked to testify in a legal proceeding.*

Records of Important Daily Events

Jot reminders about student participation, lateness to class, lack of preparation, and so on, on your lesson plan. You can write brief notes regarding student behavior and reminders of important meetings on a month-at-a-glance desk blotter block calendar. (Use abbreviations or personal codes but be sure you can decipher them.) This type of quick and easy documentation can:

- Furnish information for lesson planning.
- Provide a record of who misbehaved, when they did so, and what consequences their misbehavior incurred.
- Help you assess if behavioral guidelines are being applied consistently and fairly.
- Furnish a record of upcoming meetings and conferences as well as ones you have attended.

Notes and Reports to Administrators and Supervisors

Make copies and retain the originals of all notes, formal reports, and e-mail to administrators and supervisors and keep these in a separate file. This practice is valuable because it:

- Keeps you from having to redo misplaced paperwork.
- Helps verify that you did complete the report in question.
- Advises the recipients, especially of requests for help, that you have retained the original for your records. (Professional protocol requires that recipients be informed of all copies sent to others.)
- Supplies a prototype copy to save you time when writing a report similar in nature.
- Provides an extra copy if a child transfers to another school, the records become lost in transit, and essential information about the child is needed. (It's always a feather in your cap if you're so organized you can "bail out" others.)

Careful Documentation Equals Career Survival

Because careful documentation can help you assess if you're meeting the educational needs of your students as well as bolster any requests you might make for student support services, it is an indispensable survival skill. If you calmly and rationally request that an out-of-control child either be given extra support services or be removed from your classroom and justify your appeal with several pages of documentation, you are more likely to be taken seriously than if you storm into the office in tears and demand that a student be removed from your class because you just can't take it anymore.

If you issue a star athlete the failing grade he deserves, you will have less aggravation from the athlete's family, administrative fans, and alumnae if you document the athlete's poor academic performance, your contacts with his coach and parents, and your efforts to provide the superstar with extra help.

If you document your requests for professional guidance, additional curricular materials, and/or essential classroom furnishings by sending copies to all concerned parties and retaining the originals, you will find your requests honored more regularly and quickly than if you make spur-of-the-minute verbal requests. Such results often earn the "documenter" the reputation as a staff member who gets things done efficiently and professionally.

If you are faced with a lawsuit because a student in your care is injured while on a field trip, you will stand a much better chance of avoiding a punitive damage judgment if you have written proof that you made prudent and reasonable arrangements for your students' supervision and safety.

If you are wrongly accused by angry parents of not providing their learning disabled child with legally mandated services, you can placate them by sharing your log of the services provided their child and the child's work portfolio. If you are threatened with the loss of your job because your classes are out of control and your requests for assistance were overlooked by overwhelmed administrators, you have an excellent chance of gaining career-saving understanding and support if you have documented your past efforts to get help.

Careful Documentation Can Equal
Fewer Responsibilities

Here are three ways you can avoid being totally overwhelmed by responsibilities:

- Document the services others are to provide.
- Document your additional non-teaching responsibilities.
- Urge others to perform their assigned duties.

Document the Services Others Are to Provide

While demanding services forcefully is usually counterproductive, so too is lack of assertiveness when promised services are not forthcoming. Beginners often don't get extra help for their students because they haven't mastered the finer nuances of assuring that those services are provided. This mastery usually involves some form of documentation.

Once you learn who will provide the services a student needs and how they will provide them (see Chapter 2), document that information so everyone clearly understands his or her responsibilities. A brief note to the support person worded as follows might do the trick. For example:

I'm so glad you will be providing Sara Cross, Matt Chilcote, and Carlton Masters with extra help in reading on Mondays, Wednesdays, and Fridays from 10:00 to 11:15. Please let me know beforehand if you need to change this schedule as I have scheduled reading period for the rest of my class to coincide with your schedule.

The note must be polite, spell out the terms of the services, and indicate how failure to follow through will negatively affect your class. If scheduled services are cancelled, jot a note on your desk calendar, and should cancellations be frequent, write a note to the support person asking for a meeting to discuss the problem.

Initially it may seem easier and less time consuming just to talk with support people instead of writing them carefully worded notes. As the year progresses, however, such notes will prove well worth the extra time and effort, and once you have written one, you can use it as a prototype for others. You might even type up a form, photocopy it, and simply fill in the blanks. This documentation creates a paper trail to prove you have taken the proper procedural steps to get extra help. Support people usually have a large case-load and must prioritize (sometimes downright finagle) to get things done. By politely and professionally documenting the need for their services and their agreement to provide them, you are making your students their priorities.

Also, the majority of teachers develop a deep concern for and loyalty to those students assigned directly to them. (This doesn't mean that they don't care about the other students in the school, but their kids are . . . well . . . theirs.) So, although in most circumstances experienced teachers will go out of their way to be highly supportive of newcomers, if circumstances arise in which they must choose between one of their needy students getting extra help and one of yours, your student will seldom be their choice. Therefore, you must be prepared, if necessary, to use documentation as a tool to ensure your students receive their fair share of support services.

While it is flattering when your professional peers want you to serve as their leader, chairing a committee (or being responsible for the minutes) requires more time and effort than most beginners can afford to contribute.

Document Additional Non-teaching Responsibilities

As a member of the teaching profession you will be both required and requested to serve on various committees and to perform extra duties. You must fulfill requirements, but, depending upon who makes them, you can refuse requests.

If you are asked to serve on a committee and do not have the time nor desire to do so, put your regrets in writing. A brief note stating that you are unable to serve on the committee because of time constraints is usually enough. Remember, however, that as a member of the teaching team you must, at times, graciously volunteer to do extra work. As a beginner, the trick is not to over-volunteer or let someone over-volunteer you.

When you do serve on a committee, be sure you fully understand its purpose and your role in helping to achieve it. Document who is on the committee, its meeting dates and times, and the responsibilities of each member. This helps to ensure that there are no misunderstandings regarding this information later on. Also, if you can possibly avoid it, don't agree to serve as a committee chairperson, co-chair, or secretary. While it is flattering when your professional peers want you to serve as their leader, chairing a committee (or being responsible for the minutes) requires more time and effort than most beginners can afford to contribute.

When assigned extra duties (such as bus, cafeteria, or hall monitoring), be certain you clearly understand your responsibilities. Newcomers are often delegated extra duties, told to read the Faculty Handbook (to determine what they are supposed to do and how they are supposed to do it), only to be told by veteran teachers, "Forget about the handbook procedure because it hasn't been followed for years." Also, sometimes you will understand your role in the performance of extra duties better by observing the actions of others rather than listening to what they say.

As with committee work, document the procedures to follow for extra duties (unless the handbook procedures are valid) and the names of others assigned the same duty. It's also a good idea to record the dates you and others can't follow through, especially if there are many.

Urge Others to Perform Their Assigned Duties

At times problems arise when others are not conscientious about performing their assigned duties or continually come up with excuses for not helping out. When you feel someone is taking advantage of your better nature, take note of the times you are left "high and dry." Doing so provides perspective (sometimes we think we've been taken advantage of when, in fact, we haven't) as well as the fortitude necessary to confront the offender assertively.

Suppose that you and another new teacher are assigned afternoon bus duty along with four other experienced teachers. The two of you show up every afternoon, while one or more of the others always has some excuse as to why he or she can't be there. The experienced teachers are nice people who are (except for this bus duty problem) very supportive to you newcomers, but you feel you're being taken advantage of and want to do something about it.

> *Remember that having enough time to do everything is always*
> *a major problem for teachers.*

You can use two strategies to encourage others to perform their required duties. You can ask them for official documentation that they are excused from their responsibilities or you can document their lax performance and discuss the problem with them using the documentation as your support.

When one of the teachers announces he cannot be there for bus duty, you can state that it's okay with you as long as he has gotten someone to substitute for him. If he replies that there are enough people to take care of everything, you must politely assert that six people are assigned to bus duty because six are needed to assure student safety and calmly state that you'll be glad to try to cover the buses with only five people as long as he gets written permission from the administration for you to do so.

When another teacher fails to show up for her assigned duty for the fifth time, meet with her privately and explain that you are concerned for the safety of the students in her assigned area when she's not there. If she dismisses your concern by saying she's only missed her bus duty once or twice, you can gently inform her that according to your records she has missed it five times, and that if she continues to do so, your only recourse, because the safety of students is at issue, is to speak with the administration.

While using documentation to compel others to do their jobs seems diametrically opposed to what you've been taught about the spirit of cooperativeness found in the teaching profession, you must remember that having enough time to do everything is always a major problem for teachers. (Even when they appear to be wasting time blowing off steam in the faculty room, they are actually reducing the stress created by that third period science class which decided the bb's and straws supplied to build a hydrometer could be more creatively employed as substitute peas and peashooters.) Therefore, teachers are always prioritizing and they sometimes do so at the expense of others. Understand that this is a reality of the job and be prepared to deal with it in a manner that doesn't compromise student safety, your career, or your sanity.

Documentation, the Dual-Edged Sword

While careful documentation can provide many benefits, careless documentation can cause serious problems. It is not enough to put in writing such information as requests, behavioral records, concerns, conference notes, and so on. You must make certain that you do not put the wrong information in writing or write the right information in the wrong way. Unfortunately, if something is said, it can be glibly explained away, but if it's put in writing, there's no turning back. You should not put in writing categorical statements about students' abilities, reports containing emotionally charged words and subjective value statements, and spontaneous (and poorly considered) commitments for extra responsibilities.

Categorical Statements

Since life is uncertain, absolute statements about your students' learning and/or behavior problems and definitive proposals for dealing with them fall into the quagmire of promises that can't necessarily be kept. At best, making such statements can destroy your credibility; at worst, they may leave you open to legal action.

A report stating that a fourth grade student who is reading on a second grade level "will always remain two years behind her chronological peers" differs significantly from a report stating a fourth grader "based on the results of an informal reading inventory is testing on a second grade level and could possibly remain behind her chronological peers in reading." The former makes statements about the student's reading performance and future progress while the latter mitigates the results by allowing for the unpredictability of human growth and behavior.

Rather than definitive terms, use qualifying terms such as, "possibly," "likely," "could," or "would" when reporting about students. This indefiniteness protects you from being held accountable for setting unattainably high expectations or being blamed for making self-fulfilling prophesies about low-performance.

Subjective Statements and Emotionally Charged Words

When documenting a child's academic progress or social or emotional behavior, avoid polarizing language and value judgments and report only observable conduct. Parents, administrators, and support personnel can draw their own conclusions about the meaning of your words.

If Darryl Jackson swings his plastic lunchbox over his head lariat style and hits Ryshena Bailer on the head, report the incident just as you observed it. Do not report that Darryl Jackson was being playful, physically abusive, or "hyper." If others observed Darryl's behavior, one person might come to one of these conclusions while another might come to a different one. Therefore, report only observable behaviors. Most formal reports do, however, allow for a conclusion in which you can state your professional opinion based on the observable behaviors cited earlier in your report.

> *Rather than definitive terms, use qualifying terms such as, "possibly," "likely," "could," or "would" when reporting about students.*

For the incident chronicled above you might write, for example, "The class was returning from lunch. Ryshena Bailer was in line behind Darryl Jackson. Darryl was turned sideways standing stationary in line singing and swinging his plastic lunchbox in circles over his head. Ryshena, who was moving forward with the line, was hit in the forehead above her left eye."

Terms such as lazy, sloppy, bully, backward, clumsy, or aggressive not only reflect negatively on the child, but also on the professional who wrote the report. If you think about a student judgementally or in emotionally charged terms, ask yourself, "What behaviors do I see that lead me to this conclusion?" The answer will be observable behaviors. For example, if you conclude that a child is unmotivated, the behaviors you observe that lead you to this conclusion may be her failure to participate in class discussions, complete assignments, and hand in homework. By documenting only observable behaviors you ensure the professional integrity of your report and avoid serious problems.

Sound Advice

Keeping Your Write Stuff Organized

How you organize your documentation is a matter of personal preference. Use folders, large manila envelopes, file cabinets, or boxes to store written records. Jot notes on large-block monthly desk calendars and save each month's page in a file folder. Keep notes from parents in one specific desk drawer and notes from staff members in another. Place weekly or monthly staff bulletins under you desk blotter. Use the method that best helps you locate relevant documentation when you need it.

Notes

Chapter 10

Adapting: Bending Instead of Breaking

"Adapt or perish, now as ever, is Nature's inexorable imperative."

—H. G. Wells

Inside Chapter 10

Case Study—Ladies and Gentlemen, Change Your Schedules

Due to the delayed opening of school today, first and second period classes will not meet. All third period classes are to report to their first period subject, which will meet from 10:15 to 10:35. All fourth period classes are to report to their second period subject, which will meet from 10:40 to 11:10. Lunches will be served following the amended lunch schedule posted in each classroom. Lunch shifts will be twenty minutes in length and will begin at 10:35. The fourth lunch period is to report to the cafeteria during the first lunch period. Beginning with the second lunch period lunch shifts will follow in their proper sequential order. That is, the first lunch period is to report during second, the second during third, and the third during the fourth. Also, all A electives will meet during B elective times today. B electives will take A electives' times tomorrow.

—Morning announcement at a public high school

The Unbreakable Adaptable Teacher

In order to cope effectively with the demands of a teaching career, a beginner must be exceptionally adaptable. Proficient classroom management, human relations skills, lesson pacing, and instructional techniques all depend on appropriate and timely adjustments. Inclement weather, standardized testing, late buses, fire drills, bomb scares, assemblies, and special programs, all necessitate revisions to daily and weekly schedules. Also, the need for positive interactions with staff members, administrators, supervisors, parents, and students compels the teacher to temper his comments to assure they are accepted and acceptable. All of these adjustments call for more than a modicum of adaptability.

Stay Adaptable

When you start your first year of teaching you will generally be open-minded, accepting, and adaptable. As the year progresses, and students become more challenging, parents complain about homework and question teaching methods, and professional obligations place increased demands on time, you may find yourself seeking a magic formula to ease these pressures. You may panic and discard well-planned and balanced approaches too quickly, turning instead to those that are harsh and didactic.

Adaptability entails using an approach that addresses students' learning styles, your teaching style, and the school's philosophy of education, and modifying that approach as necessary. Flitting from one teaching approach to another is not indicative of adaptability but insecurity, and is also ineffective.

Adapt to Daily Changes

Although a wise teacher makes every effort to control the circumstances that affect his students' education, there are always those that are beyond his control. When circumstances conspire against you, be flexible enough to adjust your teaching plans accordingly. Determine beforehand some of the adjustments you might be expected to make and how you might more easily deal with them.

> *When a sudden schedule change takes place, focus on its helpfulness to you and your students.*

The Sudden Schedule Change

Sudden schedule changes are the bane of every teacher. They can result in upset, angry, and lethargic students and cause teachers to lose planning periods, miss their favorite classes, and sometimes require that they monitor students for unreasonably long periods of time. Usually caused by uncontrollable events such as inclement weather, false fire alarms, bomb scares, cancelled assemblies, and sudden teacher illness, these changes call for great flexibility and maturity on your part.

"Being prepared" is again the best way of coping with unexpected schedule changes. When planning lessons, try to think of ways they can be extended and enriched. Think of the kinds of activities you would do if time permitted; those practice activities to strengthen skills, that additional short story to improve understanding of metaphor, or the continuation of a time-shortened debate on the merits of capital punishment.

When a sudden schedule change takes place, focus on its helpfulness to you and your students. Missing that favorite class affords you the opportunity to concentrate your energies on better teaching that least adored one.

Abbreviated class periods help you better determine a lesson's main elements. (It's amazing how some of the best lessons are taught in reduced time frames because the teacher is forced to get to the heart of the matter.) Extended class periods provide extra time to improve student understanding.

You will usually view an abbreviated period more positively than an extended one because it is easier to delete parts of a lesson than to add them. (The former requires decision-making based on work that's already completed while the latter requires creative thought and renewed effort.) You can teach or review important concepts and skills during very short periods if you have considered such possibilities beforehand.

Holiday Happiness

Exceptional flexibility and patience are needed when dealing with students bathed in holiday euphoria. Elementary students are usually the most excitable followed by middle and high school students, respectively (except for some high school seniors who have mastered the art of exhibiting euphoria with an attitude). Unless you check it, student exuberance can reach the level of shrieking giddiness by the time the holiday arrives. You can control holiday-happy students by maintaining a flexible business-as-usual attitude. When a holiday activity such as a party, assembly, play, or movie is nearing, keep your students focused on educational tasks (possibly with holiday themes) until just before the activity begins. By carefully planning and executing pre-holiday lessons and gently reminding students of your behavioral expectations, you prevent them from becoming so excited and unruly that everyone's holiday is jeopardized.

 Advice

As you teach, you will notice that among the activities your students most enjoy, some are stimulating and others calming. Since sudden schedule changes inherently raise the level of excitement among students, when these changes take place, modify your lesson to include some activities that are enjoyable, stabilizing, and calming. (See page 170 for a list of some suggested activities.)

Welcoming the Unexpected New Student

Another scenario that calls for flexibility is the sudden arrival of a new student. The classroom door opens and there stands the assistant principal, guidance counselor, or student helper with a new student for your class. More than likely, your school has a definite process for admitting new students. (For example, you are to be informed of a new student a day in advance. All school records for the student must be at the school. The classroom must have an extra desk and chair to seat the student, and so on.) More than likely, however, some stressed-out person has short-circuited the process leaving you feeling shocked and frustrated. This is the time to remain calm and flexible for the sake of your new student as well as your class.

Introduce the newcomer to the class and assign a capable student who can act as a good role model to assist him throughout the day. If a desk and chair are not available, invite him to sit at yours for the remainder of the class. (Remove anything personal or confidential as you clear an area.) Ask him to complete a "Student Interest Inventory," which provides him with at least a partial respite from his feelings of awkwardness, gives your class a few moments to adjust, and provides you with an instantaneous diagnostic tool. As soon as conveniently possible thereafter, give him a copy of your expectations and behavioral guidelines and review them with him. If you keep a folder or notebook of daily class assignments, notes, and home assignments for the benefit of absentees, allow the new student to review it, and if possible, provide him with copies of this material. Also, send a note to the parents requesting that they take some time to peruse the materials given to their child. (Keep a copy of any notes to parents as suggested in Chapter 9.)

Because you know little about new students who arrive unexpectedly, treat them in a cordial yet business-like fashion. Avoid gushing over them, making physical contact with them, or putting them and the rest of your students on the spot by suspending the lesson for formal introductions (other than introducing yourself to the student and the student to the class). These well-intentioned actions often make students feel awkward and lead them to unacceptably silly behavior.

Impromptu Lessons

Surprise events sometimes provide golden opportunities to teach important but unplanned lessons. Since these lessons are impromptu and result in the postponement of required curriculum, you must be certain there are educationally sound reasons for teaching them.

Events that enhance student awareness, excitement, and, at times, even fear often result in spontaneous teachable moments. Such incidents as school emergencies (fire drills, power outages, student accidents); neighborhood events (police, fire, or health department actions); negative student interactions (arguments or fights); or natural disasters (snowstorms, hurricanes, floods, tornadoes, forest fires) can, given the proper circumstances, present you with perfect opportunities to teach lessons that address your students' curiosities, fears, and/or misperceptions.

While every exciting event might, in principle, provide teachable material, curriculum guidelines, grade level expectations, and time limits make the use of this material on a daily basis impractical. You seldom have the luxury of teaching only the material that most interests your students and are instead challenged to motivate them with the prescribed curriculum.

Surprise events sometimes provide golden opportunities to teach important but unplanned lessons.

When to Teach an Impromptu Lesson

When a sudden unusual event peaks students' interest so their desire to learn more about the topic is so strong that you are hard pressed to turn their attention to anything else, an impromptu lesson is justified.

In this case, quickly modify your teaching plan and use your students' natural interest and motivation to help them learn about whatever topic fits their needs at the time (for example, values, safety, or character education). While an impromptu lesson is usually enjoyable and informative for everyone, it should be undertaken only when certain criteria are met.

Criteria for Justifying an Impromptu Lesson

- The impromptu topic must be educational. It should, at least tangentially, be related to the curriculum, or, if not, it should touch upon important human relations issues such as student safety, behavior, or health.
- Students must learn something of value as a result of the lesson. Don't waste class time on a gripe or "bull" session.
- Students' concerns and interests must be genuine and not feigned. (The fourth period geometry class that frequently coerces their fledgling teacher into allowing them to use their math time to discuss the unfairness of their early morning lunch period, the end-of-day dismissal policy, or the policy for issuing student parking permits isn't learning geometry, but is mastering new avoidance strategies.)
- The postponement of the scheduled lesson must be because it is in your students' best interests and not because you are unprepared or unmotivated to teach the day's lesson.

The Sudden Student Behavior Decline

Regardless of how consistently and willingly a class follows behavioral guidelines or how wonderful a rapport you have built with them, at some point during the school year your class will most likely fall into a negative behavioral spiral. The convergence of more challenging subject matter, increased home assignments and long-term projects, anticipation of upcoming holidays and special events, peer pressure, and the stress of physiological growth can all contribute to a downward trend in student behavior. When you see your class turn from Dr. Jekyll to Mr. Hyde, the tendency is to try to halt the process by imposing stiffer consequences for misbehavior, implementing stringent control strategies, contacting parents, and increasing student workloads. Instead of improving, however, student behavior grows ever worse, and you, having used every conceivable weapon in your behavioral control arsenal, feel totally defeated. You search for a strategy to stop the negative behavioral spiral and restore the positive learning atmosphere to your classroom.

Halting a Negative Behavioral Spiral

As strange as it may seem, you can often bring the negative behavioral spiral to an end by relaxing behavioral consequences (with the exception of those issued for egregious behavior) and also, to a reasonable degree, by reducing the amount of work assigned to students. In other words, everyone is given amnesty, a chance to start over with a fresh slate. You should explain this change of approach during a class meeting.

Instead of teaching a regular lesson, you conduct a meeting to discuss the problem you have observed, its causes, and possible solutions. By setting clear guidelines (no name calling, blaming others, or speaking out of turn) and time limits, and gently, fairly, and patiently enforcing them, you can maintain order throughout this discussion. If students do become disorderly and rowdy, suspend the discussion until order is restored. Frequently, however, a simple reminder that you are interested in what students have to say but cannot hear or understand them when everyone is talking simultaneously, settles students enough for the discussion to continue.

Few teachers relish the image of themselves as "the enforcer," but if you fail to enforce rules or establish unenforceable rules, you will create disciplinary problems and undermine your own authority.

Once everyone shares his or her concerns and grievances and offers possible solutions, explain the amnesty procedure. Make certain that students understand it is being initiated to help everyone, you included, get back on track, and is not something you take lightly. (You want your students to get the message that you are letting them "off the hook" because they are worthy of extra understanding and trust.)

Since this approach does, however, compromise your previously stated behavioral guidelines and, therefore, to some degree, your credibility, don't use it indiscriminately but only under the most challenging of circumstances (a maximum of two or three times a year).

Adapt to the School Community
Your family and friends who are not teachers will often be mystified

Why Amnesty Works

The amnesty approach invariably results in improved student behavior and a more positive learning atmosphere because it:

- *Indicates you are willing to be flexible and work with students.*
- *Improves rapport and trust between you and your students.*
- *Helps mollify hard feelings.*
- *Models problem-solving behavior for students.*
- *Provides students with a way to end their negative behavior spiral.*

about why you are so upset that Bobby Brown didn't do his homework for the third day in a row or why you are ecstatic that Maria Wong finally understands a fraction is an equal part of a whole. They'll just smile tolerantly and ask you to pass the potatoes while you're left feeling disappointed and misunderstood. You will frequently need to vent frustrations or tout successes to those who have "been there" and genuinely understand, so a good rapport with staff members is vital to career survival.

You can develop a good rapport with your teaching peers by following a few basic human relations guidelines:

- Avoid gossip.
- Do your fair share.
- Participate in staff functions.
- Avoid interpersonal entanglements.
- Join a professional organization.

Avoid Gossip

Since even the nicest people are prone to talking about others, this is a most difficult precept to follow. As a newcomer, avoid conversations regarding the faults of others. Because you haven't been on the staff long enough to understand its integral workings (who is friends with whom, who is worthy of defense and who isn't, and so on) whatever you say in terms of gossip can easily lead to a human relations disaster.

Do Your Fair Share

To earn the respect and support of your teaching peers, you must shoulder your fair share of extra duties. Keep in mind that, as a first-year teacher, you cannot help with everything although others may encourage you to do so. Once you take on a task, however, complete it to the best of your ability, even if you realize it's the wrong one for you. If you are given the opportunity to choose your extra duties, consider the following before making your choice:

- The amount of time the duty will require—Some committees meet only a few times during the year while others meet more frequently. Important meetings may be scheduled when your workload will be heaviest such as at report card time or final exam time.
- Who will work with you—Do those who will be working with you seem reliable? (See Chapter 2.) Are there enough people to complete the task? (For example, two people aren't enough to plan and coordinate monthly school-wide assemblies, while eight to ten are more in keeping with the enormity of the task.)
- Your particular talents—During your first year, choose an activity you can do with a degree of confidence rather than try to master something new.

Participate in Staff Functions

Faculties frequently ask their members to contribute money to a fund to pay for holiday parties, gifts for departing staff members, or flowers when a death in a faculty member's family occurs. No matter how poor those college loans, car payments, rent payments, and credit card bills have left you, do your best to contribute. Sometimes you will also be asked to contribute toward gifts for wedding and baby showers, birthdays, and other special occasions. Don't feel obligated to contribute to everything, but do contribute to some.

You may be invited by your teaching peers to join them in social gatherings outside of school. These can be excellent opportunities to relax and develop long-lasting personal (as opposed to professional) friendships, but since school faculties are microcosms of society, and it's not unusual for people to exhibit different behavior at play than at work, such gatherings might provide you with more personal information about your teaching peers than you really care to know. If you find yourself at a social function where the behavior of some people makes you uncomfortable, exit gracefully and offer your regrets when similar invitations are again extended.

Avoid Interpersonal Entanglements

As a beginner, you may find yourself viewing an experienced teacher as a kind of glorified hero who can do little wrong. In return, the old pro may go on an excessive ego trip that causes her to spend more time working with and advising you than she does planning for and working with her own students. This kind of situation is detrimental to the job performance of both parties, but especially so for you because it prevents you from developing the confidence and competence you need to succeed as a teacher. So if you feel that you are becoming extremely dependent on an overly helpful colleague, pull back a bit and stand on your own two feet.

Also, almost every school has at least one Lothario who quickly sizes up the current crop of new female teachers, takes one of them under his wing, and under the guise of being helpful, tries to score with them. Often this behavior leads to nothing more than a "dance of the sexes," but it can result in serious complications, especially if Mr. Lothario is the "happily" married father of three who views his actions as fun and games, and Miss Inexperienced firmly believes they have a future together. This type of relationship is also counterproductive to the teaching careers (and sometimes the personal lives) of both parties. Again, however, it is likely to cause you more grief, because for that first year, you need to focus all of your energies on mastering the art and skill of teaching.

> *If you feel that you are becoming extremely dependent on an overly helpful colleague, pull back a bit and stand on your own two feet.*

The point is not to scare you from developing close relationships with coworkers, but to warn you of the complications that can arise from developing those relationships too quickly and intensely. Avoid problems by observing the human dynamics around you and carefully listening to the conversations that take place. Feel free to be friendly and outgoing to all, but if a staff member's attentions make you uncomfortable or you feel you are becoming overly dependent on someone for support, it may be time to distance yourself politely from that person until you are sure you are developing a relationship that will not hurt you or your career.

Join Professional Organizations

Although your time and discretionary funds may be in short supply, it is almost always in your best interest to invest at least some of these valuable commodities in membership in a professional organization. Such organizations can range from professional sororities and fraternities to specific teaching organizations (for example, the National Council of English Teachers or the National Council of Teachers of Mathematics). Also, depending on the school district, you may have the opportunity to join the local affiliate of one of the country's two largest umbrella teachers' organizations: the National Education Association or the American Federation of Teachers.

Although your time and discretionary funds may be in short supply, it is almost always in your best interest to invest at least some of these valuable commodities in membership in a professional organization.

All of these organizations hold meetings, conferences, and conventions, plus publish newsletters and periodicals to keep their members informed about current trends, research, and concerns in their fields. Local affiliates of the two largest teachers' organizations (AFT and NEA) usually negotiate the overall wage and benefits package for an entire school district and provide many additional teacher services such as liability insurance, legal advice and assistance (should you face school-related litigation), and the support of a service representative to help mediate and resolve grievance issues. Not only does joining a professional organization afford you with opportunities to stay current in your field, meet with others with similar professional interests and concerns, and participate in educational policy-making, it also enhances your feelings of professional accomplishment and pride.

Adapt to Accountability Standards

Increased accountability standards place teachers and students under greater pressure than ever before to show measurable improvement. Today teachers must pass written tests to gain and keep their certification, students must pass standardized tests to move to the next grade level, and the total school population must show marked improvement on standardized tests for the school to gain extra funding and/or to remain free from state takeover.

The fact that you must adapt your daily plans, long-term objectives, and, to some degree, teaching style to fit the goals of testing programs designed to measure the entire school's progress and also must adapt your teaching to meet the needs of each of your students, places you under great pressure and requires that you demonstrate remarkable adaptability. Regardless of what some of the "more seasoned" teachers might say, newer accountability standards are not ruining education, but they are making your overall job more challenging.

Since a school's standardized test scores can affect everything from the school's funding to the property values in its district, you will, most likely, be required to attend several workshops on how to prepare your students for the tests they will take. There are, however, some steps you can take throughout the school year to help both you and your students be better prepared at standardized test time:

- Early in the school year, review past standardized tests. If access to past tests is restricted, review the practice materials provided with them. Your department chairperson or assistant principal should have copies of these. If not, you'll probably find them (along with other useful teaching materials) in the deeper recesses of your school's book or storage rooms.
- Familiarize yourself with the test's format (multiple choice, fill in the

blanks, essay, and so on), and when feasible, prepare and administer unit tests in that format.

- Take note of terms used frequently on the test (contrast, justify, delineate, enumerate) and blend them into your daily lessons.
- Design practice exercises for your curriculum patterned after the test question format. For example, if the standardized test items require students to write an essay comparing and contrasting a topic, create a similar exercise for your students based on topics from your subject.
- Set and strictly enforce test-taking time limits. Begin by allowing students ample time to complete their work, and on subsequent practices reduce the available time.
- Practice formal testing protocol when administering some of your unit tests. Read from a script, have students move their desks away from one another, and refuse to answer questions once the test has begun.

By taking steps such as these, you ensure that you are teaching the curriculum prescribed by your school system and are also familiarizing students with the test format. Your students will not panic on test day because they will be comfortable with the test format, procedures, vocabulary, and general content.

Adapt to Certification Requirements

Most school systems require teachers to be certified to teach specific subjects and grade levels by the state board of education. The initial certification process usually consists of several steps and takes place over a period of one to three years depending on your experience and education. In order to gain certification you may be required to take additional coursework, attend workshops and seminars, and satisfactorily teach a variety of lessons that are observed and critiqued by your supervisors and administrators.

As you navigate the certification process, keep it in proper perspective. The purpose of certification is to ensure that teachers are qualified, and you, no doubt, want to be considered a qualified teaching professional. Also, in many school districts, certified teachers earn a higher salary, have the security of tenure, and can apply for promotion to supervisory and administrative positions.

Sound Advice

Although the certification process can be nerve-wracking at times, you can make it less stressful by:

- *Obtaining and reviewing the certification guidelines for your school district.*
- *Limiting the number of elective workshops and inservice courses you take to one or two a semester.*
- *Choosing elective workshops and inservice courses that present practical (instead of theoretical) information.*
- *Avoiding commitments for postgraduate work until after your first year of teaching if possible.*

Adapt to Career Realities

Those starting a career in education must adjust to certain realities and anomalies inherent to the teaching profession. Among these are:

- The work day in no way ever resembles six and a half hours. While you may have observed teachers leaving their schools along with the children at the end of the day, it was not to go home and forget about their jobs.
- Almost all of those vacation days (especially summer ones) are used for professional development (such as coursework required to gain or maintain certification) or committee work and preparation for the next school year, most of which is required "volunteer" work.
- Telephone calls during the school day that take more than ten minutes are out of the question because of your schedule.
- Leaving the building during your duty-free time is out of the question unless you have nerves of steel and a lead accelerator foot. . . There's never enough time to get there and back without being late for your next class.
- Restroom needs must coincide perfectly with planning periods. Otherwise, you must rely on your teaching neighbor to monitor both his class and yours while you address nature's call. This is also true for any sudden bout of illness. If you feel ill, you must be sure to get someone to cover for you before you leave your classroom.

- A special set of lesson plans must be prepared and left on file in case you are ill or have an emergency. Some school districts require teachers to find their own substitutes. In certain circumstances (for example, the plans you have on file don't cover the necessary material, or, worse yet, you have no plans on file), an absence can mean dragging yourself out of bed, planning a lesson, and taking it to school.
- Faculty meetings, at times, become extended marathons as staff members argue the merits (replete with personal anecdotes) of such important matters as whether it's better to have students line up in the cafeteria or in the hall outside the cafeteria.

Human dynamics require great tact and sensitivity since:
- Parents do not deal well with straightforward unvarnished criticisms of their children and can make your life a living hell should you be unwise enough to offer them.
- Administrators view straightforward and unvarnished criticisms of their administrative style and practices the same as parents do of their children.
- Fellow teachers view straightforward and unvarnished criticisms of their teaching style and practices the same as parents do of their children and administrators do of their administrative practices.

The best advice for when you are ready to throw in the towel is, "don't," but instead, hang on for a little longer.

What to Do if You Have Trouble Adapting

As the school year progresses, there will be times when things will move along quite well and you will feel very satisfied with the progress you and your students are making. There will also be times when you will question why you ever wanted to be a teacher in the first place.

You may notice that just when things are going very badly and you're ready to take a job selling shoes or washing cars, they suddenly take a turn for the better. So, the best advice for when you are ready to throw in the towel is, "don't," but instead, hang on for a little longer.

Generally, after a period of careful observation and hard work, you will learn the accepted methods of implementing your school system's educational program (what you really must and must not do as opposed to the philosophy that is espoused for public relations purposes). You will adapt your teaching approach to fit the guidelines set by your school and school district and fashion your interpersonal relationships to meet the expectations of your fellow teaching professionals.

If you try as hard as you possibly can for your entire first year and still have serious difficulty controlling your students and teaching satisfactory lessons, take heart; you are not the first beginning teacher to ever be in such a position. Many teachers have problems adjusting to the considerable demands placed on them during their initial year of teaching, and yet strengthen their resolve, learn from their mistakes, and do very well thereafter.

Some teachers get off to a rocky start in one school or school district, transfer to another, and have few problems after that. Frequently this happens because there is a better match between the expectations of the school or school district and the capabilities of the teacher. Sometimes, when all else fails, a change may lead to success.

Notes

Chapter 11

Persisting: Keeping on Keeping on

*"Nothing in the world can take the place of persistence.
Talent will not; . . . Genius will not; . . . Education will not; . . .
Persistence and determination alone are omnipotent."*

—Calvin Coolidge

 **Chapter 11**

Case Study—Mr. Aziz Persists

It is the first week of school and Mr. Aziz's fourth period vocal music class enters the room in a loud and disorganized manner. There is pushing and shoving, thrown pencils, raucous laughter, and shouting. Mr. Aziz waits until most of the students are seated and then calmly directs the others to be seated. He then asks his students to tell him the procedures for entering the music room. Once the procedures are reviewed, he directs his class to return to the hall and enter his room in the appropriate manner, taking care not to disturb the other classes that are in session.

This time when they enter their behavior is much better, but still leaves room for improvement. Mr. Aziz calmly and patiently refuses to allow his students to enter the room unacceptably. On their third attempt, the class enters appropriately. Mr. Aziz compliments them for doing so, and begins the lesson. At the end of class, he reminds his students of the behavior he expects them to exhibit whenever they enter his room.

Persistence: The Vital Link to Career Success

If flexibility is necessary for your survival, persistence is vital for your overall success. If you want a long and successful career in education you must persevere at mastering the basic skills and fine nuances of teaching. You cannot turn tail and run should your evaluation be less than stellar, your students challenge your authority, some parents complain you are too easygoing while others complain you are Attila the Hun, your colleagues vote you chairman of the student assembly committee and leave you to arrange

To be a successful teacher you must persist in several ways. You must be determined to:
- Stay focused.
- Keep a positive attitude.
- Seek better ways to reach your students.
- Maintain self-control.
- Have an excellent attendance record.
- Keep everything in perspective.

all of the assemblies (single-handedly), and the school custodian refuses to vacuum the floor in your classroom because you forget to direct your students to put their chairs up at the end of hectic and challenging days.

Stay Focused

Stay so strongly focused on educating students that everything else is peripheral and of little consequence. Your main job is to help children learn and, if you do that well, everything else will fall into place. While you cannot disregard all that is peripheral, it helps to focus on your main priority.

Keep a Positive Attitude

Keep a positive attitude and don't allow your professional judgment to be clouded by students' negative comments (especially if you teach middle or high school students.) Although you would obviously prefer all of your students to be happy with you all the time, this is impossible given the nature of your job. Sometimes you will make mistakes and some student complaints will be warranted, so you will need to adjust your teaching style as well as your academic and behavioral expectations in your students' best interests.

Seek Ways to Reach Students Better

Plan the day's lessons diligently and note areas of student confusion as you teach. Do not give up when your students "just don't get it," but search for other methods of presentation and alternative techniques to help them. When frustrated by unmotivated students, lack of parental support, or increasing demands on your time, refuse to play the "blame game," but instead, strive to remain objective and seek ways to circumvent these common concerns.

Don't keep raising your voice louder and louder in order to be heard over an increasing din of inattentive students talking among themselves.

Maintain Self-Control

Maintain self-control and expect your pupils to do the same. Your students will feel secure when working with you because you are calm and patient, and the few times you are not, they will know their behavior is totally unacceptable. Don't keep raising your voice louder and louder in order to be heard over an increasing din of inattentive students talking among themselves. Instead, patiently and unemotionally insist that students follow reasonable behavioral guidelines and refuse to allow unacceptable behavior to obstruct education in your classroom. Do this not only by using good teaching and behavioral control techniques, but also by exercising your own force of will. Enter the classroom every day well prepared and determined to teach to the best of your ability, and your students will note your resolve and assent to your leadership.

Have an Excellent Attendance Record

Have an excellent attendance record. Students need stability and consistency in order to learn well. Don't stay home with the covers pulled over your head after a difficult day, but instead muster your courage and head for school more determined than ever that your students will behave and will learn. Know that every problem you face presents you with not only an opportunity to learn and grow, but also a chance to engender solutions that may be helpful to everyone.

It is very difficult, if not downright impossible, to be consistently kind, understanding, and upbeat with your students if you are not kind and understanding with yourself.

Keep Things in Perspective

Persist at keeping things in perspective as you progress through your initial year of teaching. Learn as much as you can about your students and your school and then plan lessons to address your students' needs within the parameters of your school's educational philosophy and power structure.

Persist in implementing your plans but remain sensitive to student feedback and make adjustments accordingly. Set realistic behavioral standards and consistently demand that they be met. Deal with behavior problems in a straightforward steadfast fashion and communicate your concerns and praise to others in the same manner. Persist in keeping thorough documentation and in seeking help and support when you perceive it is necessary. Most importantly, persist in keeping everything in its proper perspective.

Remember that it is very difficult, if not downright impossible, to be consistently kind, understanding, and upbeat with your students if you are not kind and understanding with yourself. Be certain to squeeze some genuine "down time" (time to pursue interests totally unrelated to your job) into your busy schedule, and strive to keep your sense of humor since the ability to laugh not only reduces stress but also adds great joy to life. Keep in mind, especially as those first year's pressures grow, that your ultimate role is not to teach a beautiful lesson to impress the "powers that be," nor to make students hop to attention to demonstrate your power over them, nor to zip through the year's curriculum more quickly than any other teacher to prove that you are the most efficient teacher on the staff. Your paramount role is to help children master the skills and acquire the information they need to become responsible and productive adults.

Notes

Appendix A

Some Answers to Beginners' Questions

But I Still Have Questions!

If you have questions about specific teaching problems, bear in mind there are no fail-safe answers. Viable solutions to your specific concerns must match the set of dynamics unique to an individual student's personality/learning style, a specific class' collective personality/learning style, your personality/teaching style, and the rules of your school system. Teachers in general, however, often employ some relatively simple strategies to deal with typical teaching problems. Some of these are discussed below.

Pupils without Pencils

A few of my students constantly come to mathematics class without pencils. If the other students or I lend them pencils, not only do we rarely get them back, but also the borrowers then rely on us to supply them daily. How can I get my students to come to class with their own writing materials?

Students who constantly do not have a pencil (or pen) are a source of teacher concern and frustration. If you provide these materials, you risk reinforcing irresponsible behavior, and if you don't, you undermine your goal of helping students learn. Therefore, you must use strategies that strongly encourage students to bring their own supplies and discourage them from relying on others. Some of these are:
- The Zero Pencil Equals Zero Grade Policy
- The Pencil Pot Procedure
- The Loan Secured by Collateral Strategy
- The Purchase a Pencil Plan

The Zero Pencil Equals Zero Grade Policy
Some experienced teachers establish a "no pencil (or pen) = no work = zero grade" rule. Such a rule, however, can lead to frustrated, angry, and idle students. If you tell students at the beginning of a class that, regardless of how well they do, their grade is a zero, they often lose motivation and become difficult to manage.

The Pencil Pot Procedure

A less perilous approach is to create a "pencil pot." Collect all the old, discarded, and scuzzy pencils you can find, put them in a container, and distribute them as "loaners." Since most students dislike using derelict writing tools, having to borrow from the pencil pot encourages them to bring their own supplies. A variation of this strategy (useful with older students) is to distribute only large fat primary pencils as loaners. If you use this variation, be sure to implement it in a low-keyed, matter-of-fact, business-like fashion that spares the borrower embarrassment.

The pencil pot offers a solution to the missing pencil problem, but it also creates a few problems of its own. Students can waste much valuable class time choosing the best of the worst from the pencil pot, and when there are several borrowers in the same class, they can cause the teacher to waste much valuable teaching time monitoring the pencil pot. Sympathetic students who rush to aid the hapless borrower can also cause problems. Over-exuberant peer helpfulness can lead to pencils being thrown across the room, several students jumping up and running about the room to provide their classmate with a pencil simultaneously, or the borrower moving from lender to lender to determine who has the best loaner merchandise.

Avoid the picky-borrower problem by insisting that those borrowing from the pencil pot accept whatever pencil is handed them. Prevent "sympathetic classmate pandemonium" by prohibiting the borrowing and lending of supplies (except from the teacher) once the lesson is underway. If your class has serious behavior problems, you might prohibit borrowing in the classroom at any time to prevent lesson-destroying feuds about whose supplies belong to whom, who "stole" what from whom, or who took someone's "good stuff" and lent it to an unsuspecting borrower.

The Secured Loan

The loan secured by collateral requires the borrower to provide you with something of value for use of the loaner pencil. When the student returns the pencil, you return the collateral. (It is unwise to accept anything of great value as collateral.) Depending on the maturity of your students and the rapport you have with them, you may require specific collateral (for example, a shoe or baseball cap), but any collateral you receive should be witnessed by others and kept in a safe place. The loan secured by collateral usually works well with older students and is useful in teaching them important laws of finance. For it to work well, however, you must employ it in a good humored and courteous manner.

The Purchase a Pencil Plan

The teacher purchases pencils and sells them to unprepared students at cost. The purchase plan requires a backup plan to deal with students who can't afford or don't want to buy a pencil. Also, it can cause some students to rely on you as their pencil retailer. A variation of the purchase plan useful with some younger students is to request the parents of the constantly unprepared student to provide you with a supply of pencils for their child. When the child needs a pencil, you give her one. Use this variation with great care, however, since it can easily reinforce irresponsibility.

Students Who Need Extra Test-Taking Time

A student in my sixth grade science class works so slowly that she finishes only half the items on her science tests. Most of the work she completes is correct, but she finishes so little that all of her test grades are unsatisfactory. I would like somehow to modify her tests so they give a fairer picture of her achievement, but I honestly don't have the time to design a special test for just one student. Is there an easier solution?

There are a few simple ways you can modify tests and test procedures so the results indicate the slower test-taker's understanding of the material. The one you use depends on the needs of the student and the dynamics unique to your teaching situation. You can provide extra test-taking time, grade only the test items the student completes, or select specific items for completion.

Provide Extra Test-taking Time

The easiest solution for this problem is to give the student the extra time needed to complete her test, but curriculum guidelines, teaching schedules, and classroom dynamics often make this solution impractical. If you do manage to provide extra test-taking time for one student, in the interest of fairness, you must, with few exceptions, give additional time to all who request it. Since this can easily become a logistical and public relations nightmare, a better solution is to adjust the length of the test instead of allowing students more time to take it. You can do this by grading only the completed test items or selecting a sampling of test items to grade.

Grade Only the Test Items the Student Completes

Evaluate only the number of items the slower test-taker actually completes. If she completes four problems and gets three correct, she earns a grade of seventy-five percent (three out of four). While this modification is easy to implement, it does not always provide fair and accurate test scores. When the test has a wide variety of problems or problems that progress from easy to difficult, those the student completes may not be indicative of her understanding of all of the concepts being assessed.

Selecting Specific Items for Completion

You can modify a test to indicate more fairly the slower test-taker's understanding of the concepts it covers by selecting specific items for her to complete. You might, for example, require her to complete items 1, 3, 4, 8, 10, 16, 17, 19, and 20 since those items best indicate mastery of the most important concepts on the test. (By requiring the test-taker to complete a few more items on each successive test, you can help the student increase her work speed.) When you select a sampling of items, instruct the student to complete the selected items first and then complete as many additional items as time permits. This keeps everyone working during the allotted time and also short-circuits complaints about unfairness from the rest of the class.

There are several ways you can present this test modification to your students. You can:

- List the numbers of the first-to-be-completed test items on the board.
- Mark the required items on the students' test papers prior to administering the test.
- Go to each student (once the test is under way) and check off the

items they are to complete. This "on-the-spot" individualizing can also be useful for reducing test-taking anxiety in new students and students returning from long-term absences. You can discreetly direct the anxious student to complete only the less challenging test items. If these items prove too difficult, you can give the student a less challenging test from your file of previous tests. If none of these solutions seems appropriate, you can pencil in some less challenging problems on the student's test paper or excuse her from completing the test.

The Excessively Inquisitive Student

A student in my tenth grade American History class is always asking questions that have already been answered or are totally unrelated to the lesson. It has gotten so that everyone in the class groans when I call on him. I want to encourage inquiry, but I'm concerned that too much class time is being lost on unnecessary and frivolous questions. How can I stop this student from asking so many unnecessary questions without creating a negative learning environment?

Before attempting to stop this student's many inquiries, it's important to consider what might be motivating him to ask so many questions. Is it possible he has a hearing impairment? Is he genuinely confused? Is he asking questions to gain attention? Is he manipulating class dynamics to gain power and control?

Speak with other teachers to find out if he behaves the same way in their classes. If not, ask them for some pointers on managing his constant queries, keeping in mind there are differences between one teacher's classroom dynamics and another's. If other teachers are having a similar problem, your next step should be a visit to the school nurse or health records files to find out if your questioner has a hearing or other physiological problem that might cause him to ask so many redundant questions. If, because of some strange communications snafu, he has a documented physiological problem of which his teachers weren't informed, you must make the appropriate modifications to enable him to learn in your classroom. You might, for instance, seat him where he can better hear and see what is being said, write the main points of the lesson on the board without fail, and keep background noise to a minimum when presenting the main points of the lesson.

If the questioner's behavior has no physiological cause, limit the number of questions he is permitted to ask during a class period. Meet privately with the student and explain that while you want him to feel free to ask questions during class, his many questions are making it difficult for you to cover the required curriculum. Tell him that you must limit him to three (or another reasonable number) questions a class, but he may, however, write down any others and meet with you at a mutually agreeable time to have those questions answered. This strategy is helpful because it:

- Limits the amount of class time the questioner can monopolize.
- Causes the questioner to reflect on the importance of a question and helps him set questioning priorities.
- Provides the questioner with the opportunity, should he choose to take it, to have all of his questions answered and have your undivided attention.
- Does not discourage other students from asking questions.

Inappropriate Student Behavior in an Informal Setting

As a first year middle school physical education teacher, I'm not sure how to relate to students and manage their behavior in less formal setting such as intramurals or after school sports clubs. I know kids participate in extra-curricular activities to have fun and don't want an uptight drill-sergeant supervising them, but when I lighten things up by joking and teasing with them, they seem to forget I'm their teacher and begin treating me as one of their peers. They pound me hard on the back, make gestures behind my back, play keep-away with the equipment, and parrot back what I say. How do I stop this kind of behavior without seeming like a bad sport? How do I know when to tighten up and when to lighten up?

New teachers, especially those with chronological ages close to those of their students, are frequently concerned about just how congenial to be. Most have heard veteran teachers' admonitions, "Don't smile for the first month of school. Be very strict in the beginning of the year and loosen up later. It's easier to loosen up than tighten up." Regardless of how harsh such advice seems or how much it contradicts the more idealistic approaches to teaching and discipline presented in education courses, it is somewhat sound. Highly emotional students often present complex teaching challenges that are difficult for the average beginner to manage, and overly agreeable or disagreeable teachers elicit strong emotions from their students. Avoid becoming best buddies (or worst enemies) with your students. Do this by earning and keeping their respect, and since respect is a two way street, in most cases, you will get as good as you give.

You earn respect in the classroom by establishing appropriate behavioral guidelines and consistently and fairly enforcing them. In less structured settings such as after school clubs, sporting activities, school dances, and parties, however, you may be uncertain about what guidelines to establish. Unfortunately, this uncertainty can cause a downward behavioral spiral. Your uncertainty leads to student uncertainty, student uncertainty leads to testing (to determine exactly what is permissible), and testing often leads to unacceptable behavior.

When working with students informally, you must rely on your personal comfort level to guide you in setting behavioral standards. If student behavior makes you feel uncomfortable, it is most likely unacceptable, and you must confront it.

Confronting Without Being Confrontational

If only one or two students are misbehaving, confront them individually, but if the majority of the group is behaving poorly, address everyone. Raise your voice loudly enough to gain everyone's attention, ignore any wisecracks or disrespectful remarks that may be made, and in a well-modulated authoritative voice calmly state your case. Be sure your comments convey the message that:

- You care about your students and don't want to see them get hurt.
- You care about the property of others and don't want to see it damaged.
- You are a mature adult and intend to act and be treated as such.

You might say, for example, "I know you are all here to have fun, and I want you to do so, but, as your teacher and the person responsible for your safety and conduct, I can't allow you to engage in dangerous, destructive, or disrespectful behavior. So from now on the following behaviors will not be tolerated. . ."

Your Comfort Level is the Key

To determine just how amiable to be with students in informal settings, have confidence in your own judgment and personal comfort levels. If in your judgment students are exhibiting poor behavior, trust your experience and act quickly to end such behavior, but take care to do so in a low-keyed professional manner.

An Intimidating Instructional Assistant

One of the greatest causes of stress for me as a beginning teacher is my instructional assistant. She's worked at this school forever, knows all of the kids and their parents, and seems to disapprove of everything I do. To make matters even worse, when she is in my classroom, my kids see her as the authority and not me. How do I deal with this situation?

You and your instructional assistant are not competitors but partners in the education business. As teacher, you are responsible for the educational program in your classroom. Your job, on its most fundamental level, is to teach a prescribed curriculum to students, and your instructional assistant, regardless of how much experience she has, is there to help you.

If, however, you are fortunate enough to have an experienced instructional assistant who knows the parents, children, and school, take advantage of her experience and knowledge. You might seek her thoughts on seating arrangements (who works best with whom), which parents will be most supportive of special projects, how best to get that burned-out light replaced, and how to deal with Leena Patel's constant chatter. (You, of course, must be the judge of how to use this information.)

When working with your students, patiently and consistently enforce your behavioral standards and classroom procedures, and direct your instructional assistant to do the same. If she does and the children respond to her before they respond to you, don't view their behavior as a personal affront. Instead, concentrate on the positive outcome: students are following the rules and procedures. Regardless of what may be happening around you or how insecure you feel, if you always focus on teaching your students, you will always be doing your job. It's hard for anyone in a school to disapprove of a teacher who is always doing his or her job.

The Disorganized Class

My third grade students are very messy. Their materials spill over onto each other's desks and the floor around them. Their desks are crammed full of crumpled up papers. They are so poorly organized that they can't find anything when they need it. When I direct them to take out certain classwork papers or workbooks, they rummage around seemingly forever. When I use class time for clean up, within a day or so everything is messy again. It bothers me to keep wasting teaching time on clean ups. What can I do to manage this mess?

In general, children with good organizational skills learn more efficiently than those without them, but most children need guidance to acquire these skills. Since your students undoubtedly have poor organizational skills, you must (within the constraints of your prescribed curriculum guidelines) not only take the time to help them get organized, but also show them ways to stay organized. Here are a few suggestions that might help:

- Limit the number of things students can have in their desks at any time. For example, no more than four pencils, two pens, an eraser, a ruler, a notebook, and five papers may be kept in students' desks; everything else is to be stored in a specified area in the classroom.
- Schedule a weekly cleaning session and adhere to it faithfully.

- Have inspections of desks and storage areas before recess and dismissal.
- Prohibit students from using their desks as wastebaskets; they may not keep crumpled up papers in their desks.
- Have a student volunteer collect the paper trash at scheduled times throughout the day.
- Provide color-coded folders made from colored construction paper for each subject. For example, have blue for reading, red for math, yellow for science, and so forth.
- If students need more storage space to stay organized, provide each with a cardboard box for extra storage (covering and decorating these can be a fun activity).

The Overly Tired Working Student

A student in my first period calculus class frequently falls asleep during class. I know from speaking with him about this problem that he has a job after school and is saving to buy a car. He's promised to cut back on his work hours and begged me not to tell his parents because they'll make him quit his job. His grades are falling, and I know his parents will figure out the cause when they see his report card. He's a really nice young man, and I hate to cause him problems and destroy his trust in me. What do I do?

Step back and view this problem objectively, and ask yourself some hard questions. If this young man were your son, would you (regardless of the job aspect) expect his teacher to inform you that he is frequently falling asleep in your class? Is there a possibility this young man could fall asleep driving to or from his job? Is it possible that the job is not the cause of his sleeping in class, but he might have a drug or alcohol problem? Is his employer breaking child labor laws? What are you going to tell the parents if they ask why their son's calculus grades have fallen?

Your answers to questions such as these should help you understand that you have little choice but to inform the parents. Before you do so, speak with the student privately, inform him of your decision, explain your reasoning, and offer to meet with him and his parents to discuss the problem. When you deliver this news, however, be prepared to face an angry and disappointed young man and try not to take what he says at this time personally.

A Rigid Principal

Many of the newer teachers at my school disagree with our principal's rigid disciplinary style. When students break a rule, even if there are extenuating circumstances, he shows them no mercy. Two boys were thrown off the junior varsity football team because they were at a party where some other kids were drinking alcohol, and a girl was suspended because she gave her best friend Tylenol for a headache. These are just two examples of his "by the book" style!

A group of us met with him and shared our concerns, but he was intractable. He listened politely and made comments that indicated he understands our concerns. ("You think I enforce the school district's policies too harshly and want me use a more compassionate approach.") At the end of the meeting, he thanked us for sharing our concerns and told us that, while he respected our views, his job is to enforce the school district's policies as written and he intends to do just that. How can we convince him to be a little more flexible?

Since you have told him about your concerns, there's little else you can do. It's the principal's job to deal with the major disciplinary issues at your school, but keep in mind, you probably don't know all of the facts surrounding his actions. You can, however, make certain your students are keenly aware of the school's disciplinary policies, especially the consequences for rule infractions. Also, regardless of how strongly you feel about this issue, avoid developing an "us versus him" attitude. It can easily create a contentious and negative learning environment and cause you to be labeled a troublemaker, a label that can stick for many years to come.

The Recurrent Restroom User

A child in my class visits the restroom at least ten times every day. When questioned about her behavior, she acts embarrassed and says she really needs to use the restroom. Her requests are so frequent that the other children are beginning to make fun of her. How do I deal with this problem?

Granting a child permission to use the restroom seems like a foregone conclusion, but some children use restroom privileges as an escape mechanism. As a result, indiscriminately allowing some students to use the restroom can be detrimental to their education. Before limiting any child's restroom visits, however, you must speak with the school nurse, and you may want to speak with her previous teachers and her parents.

Check with the school nurse to see if the child has a medical problem. If she does, she must have access to the restroom, and you can tactfully explain this to your class. If there is no physical reason to excuse her frequently, you can simply limit the number of times you permit her to leave your classroom. This will check her sojourns, but won't reveal what motivates them. If you wish to discover this, you must investigate more extensively.

Discuss the problem with her previous teachers and her parents to get their thoughts on her behavior and their suggestions for dealing with it. This may give you greater insight into the child's motivation for leaving and provide you with viable methods for dealing with her behavior. If not, you can make your own behavioral analysis.

For a week or two note what your class is doing when the child asks to be excused. (You can jot this information on your lesson plan or your desk blotter.) Then, review your notes looking for behavioral patterns. (For example, she always leaves when oral reading or class discussions take place or after she completes her independent practice sheets or whenever homework is reviewed.) Next, meet with the child privately and discuss your observations. You might say, "Janie, I'm concerned because you spend so much time out of the classroom that you miss important parts of the lesson. I've noticed that you leave whenever the class breaks into small groups. Is there something happening within these groups that I might be able to help you with?" Your attention and genuine concern will usually motivate the child to tell you the cause of her behavior, and once you know the cause, you can work to eliminate it. If your meeting with the child proves fruitless, you can explain to her that you must limit her trips from your room but are willing to talk with her again when she feels ready to do so.

The Money Borrower Problem

The children in my class frequently ask to borrow lunch money, and I hate to refuse because I don't want them to go hungry. The problem is they aren't very good about paying me back, and I'm going broke feeding the multitudes. How can I get my students to pay me back when they borrow money from me?

A teacher is under no obligation to lend students money and can simply refuse to do so. Since, however, teachers and the school administration don't want children to go hungry, most schools use less harsh methods to deal with the lunch-money borrower.

Some schools have a petty cash fund from which they make loans to children. Find out if your school has such a fund, and if so, make use of it. Other schools issue a small fund to teachers to use for student emergencies. It's possible your school does this, and through oversight, you haven't received your emergency fund. If your school doesn't make such funds available, and you wish to provide loans to students, you must set some guidelines for doing so.

When you lend them money, have students give you a dated and signed I.O.U. Keep all I.O.U.'s on file. When a student repays you, give him back his I.O.U. Establish a rule that you will not lend money to anyone who has an outstanding I.O.U. and be sure to enforce it consistently. By establishing and enforcing this rule you are helping children understand the importance of paying their debts and establishing good credit. Invest in a supply of snack foods such as peanut butter and crackers to offer those students who, because they haven't paid their debts, might go hungry.

Appendix B

Sample Charts and Forms

Sample Student Information Note-Taking Form

Student's Name: _____ D.O.B. _____ Phone # _____

Address _____ Country of Origin (if not USA) _____

Citizenship: _____ Primary language _____ ESOL _____

Parents'/Guardians' Names: _____

Relationship: _____

Work phone # _____ Adoption: _____ Foster parents: _____ Since: _____

Student's health: Glasses: _____ Hearing aid: _____ Physical handicap: _____

Medication(s) that affect learning/behaviors _____ What: _____

Special needs student: _____ Handicapping condition: _____

Known behavior problems: _____

Suspended from school: _____ Number of times: _____ Notes: _____

Test Records

Type	Results	Name of Test	Notes
I.Q.			
Reading Rec.			
Reading Comp.			
Math			

Last year's teacher(s): _____ Subject(s): _____

Number of schools student has attended: _____

Hobbies, interests: _____

Parental Support: Very supportive: _____ Supportive _____ Non-Supportive: _____

Additional Notes: _____

Teacher/Staff Interview Note Form

Staff member: _____   Date of interview: _____

Student Name	Seating Suggestions	Useful Academic Techniques	Useful Behavioral Techniques	Notes, Observations

Sample Parent Contact Note Form

Student	Parent/Guardian Contacted	Date	Phone #	Comments/Questions For Parent	Parent Responses

Sample Phone Log

Date	PID*	TOC**	Name of Person	Concerning	Resolution	*Person I.D. P = Parent/Guardian Pr = Principal Ap = Assistant Principal S = Social Worker T = Other teacher Sup = Supervisor M = Mentor U = Union Rep. D = Doctor (med) O = Other	**Type of Call 1 = Information gathering 2 = Information sharing 3 = Parent conference 4 = Complaint 5 = Apology 6 = Other

Furniture Arrangement Floor Plans

(See page 166 for explanations.)

4

5

6

Furniture Arrangement Floor Plans (continued)

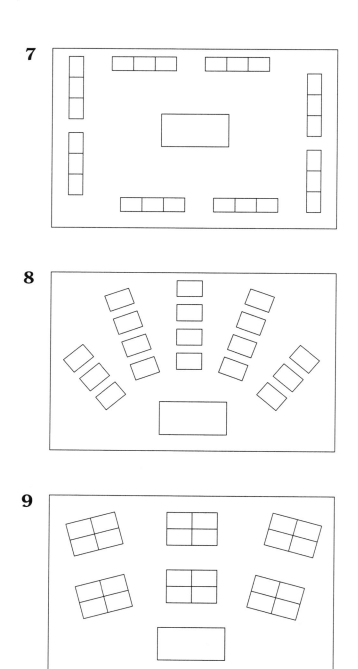

Furniture Arrangement Floor Plans (continued)

10

11

12

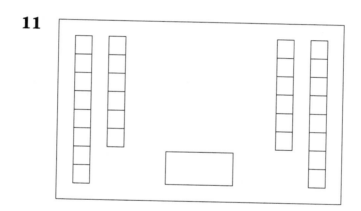

Advantages and Disadvantages of Seating Arrangements Shown on Pages 162 through 165

#	Advantages	Disadvantages
1	Minimizes interaction among students; directs focus to the front of the room.	Discourages student discussion; uses a great deal of floor space.
2	Promotes interaction and discussion between partners.	Not conducive to larger grouping; interaction between partners can be negative.
3	Promotes discussion among students in the group; useful for small group activities.	As many as half of the students can have their backs turned to the teacher and main teaching area; promotes discussion among students in the group.
4	Same as for #3.	Chalkboards visible to all students but only at an uncomfortable angle for some.
5	Separates students into large groups; enhances class debate and discussion.	Encourages students to call across the classroom to one another; materials from one student can easily overflow into another student's area.
6	Student focus drawn to front of room; saves floor space.	Inhibits discussion among the group members; materials from one student can easily overflow into another student's area.
7	Conducive to class discussions; students' focus is on one another.	Student focus is not always on the teacher when it should be; one group has its back to the chalkboard and main teaching area.
8	Interaction of students minimized; teacher can easily see and have access to each student; discourages cheating during tests.	Discourages student interaction; hard to keep desks in their proper alignment; takes a great deal of floor space.
9	Promotes discussion and allows for grouping.	Students face one another so some have their backs to the teacher; encourages talking among students.
10	Minimal interaction among students; focus on center of the room; useful for testing.	Teacher will always have his/her back to several students; some students will always have their backs to the chalkboard/main teaching area.
11	Division of class into two distinct teams; useful for debates or competitions; saves floor space.	Promotes a "them versus us" attitude; materials from one student can easily overflow into another student's area.
12	Promotes interaction between members of a large group; saves floor space.	Talking among the members of the large groups can be difficult to control; students must always focus at an angle to see the boards.

Sample Interest Inventory

The following is a sample of some of the questions that you might use to gather information about your students. The inventory, just as everything else in teaching, must be geared to the ability level of students. Give primary classes the least challenging questions (possibly requiring only a one word answer or a selection from a list) and give high school students the most challenging questions.

Name:_____Date:_____

Interest Inventory

1. What school subject do you like best? _____

   What about this subject do you like most? _____

   _____

2. What subject do you like least? _____

   What about this subject do you like least?_____

   _____

3. What is your favorite color? _____

4. What is your favorite sport? _____

5. Who is your favorite athlete?_____

6. What kinds of music do you like best? _____

7. Who is your favorite musician/band?_____

8. Who is your favorite movie star?_____

9. What is your favorite movie? _____

   What about it do you like the most? _____

10. Who in your family do you admire the most? _____

    What about this person do you most like? _____

_____

11. Who is your hero?_____

12. How should a hero behave? _____

13. What is your favorite television show?_____

14. What kinds of pets do you have? _____

15. What amusement park ride do you enjoy the most?_____

16. What is your favorite book? _____

    What part in that book did you like best? _____

    _____

17. What do you think is your greatest talent? _____

18. If you could change one thing about yourself, what would it be? _____

    _____

19. What is the best time you have ever had? _____

    _____

20. If you were given three wishes, what would you wish for? _____

    _____

    _____

Sample Strategic Seating Arrangement

Desks (student names with strategic notes):

- Empty ⑧ | Tony Martin
- Alan James | Manuel Woods
- Kary Markam | Allen Amar ⑨
- Alice Truesdale | Mary Norris
- Rowlewa Green | Tamika Blake
- Tracy Bonner | Torell Ceroni
- Benson Cheng | Ian Petchek
- Thomas James | Soon Li
- Inez Perez | William Miller
- Kevin Kunkle | Ben Swartz
- Pavel ⑥ Ivanovich | Jovan Walls ⑦
- Susan ① Howard | Juan Hernandez
- Darwan Brown | Sam Smoot ②
- Jan Friedman | Andrei Demidenko ⑤
- Amanda Sims ③ | Tiffany Borden ④
- Henri Boulby | Penny Pace

Teacher's Desk

Legend:

1. Student with a sight problem.
2. Student who needs individual attention
3. Student who is extremely talkative.
4. Student who is very shy and quiet.
5. Good student who speaks both Russian and English.
6. Newly immigrated Russian student.
7. Talkative student
8. Empty desk.
9. Hyperactive student.

Additional Calming Activities

- Taking a test or quiz

- Doing cross number puzzles

- Connecting the dots

- Figuring out mazes

- Cutting and pasting (food groups; pictures of cars, insects, trees, flowers, and so on; a picture for each letter of the alphabet)

- Practicing multiplication (writing out multiplication tables)

- Alphabetizing practice

- Practicing numerical order (organizing numbers: least to greatest or greatest to least)

- Practicing handwriting

- Organizing notebooks or portfolios

- Writing lists (all the characters in a story, people in the classroom, and so on)

- Illustrating a story

- Reading (anything appropriate)

- Writing a story, poem, song, story, letter, play, e-mail

- Creating a collage or scrapbook (animals, insects, children, cars, sports, clothing styles, and so on)

- Creating as many smaller words as possible using letters from a larger word

- Drawing a floor plan of school, home, church, and so on

- Drawing a map of the community around school or home

- Filling in blank maps with the names of states, nations, continents, oceans, rivers
- Looking up and writing the meanings of vocabulary words
- Designing a book or album cover
- Journal writing
- Outlining chapters from a text
- Summarizing a newspaper article
- Writing a letter to the editor, a parent, the school principal
- Comparing and contrasting two articles on the same subject
- Writing a class history

Field Trip Checklist Example

The following is an example of a checklist that you might use to be sure that you have prepared thoroughly for a field trip. Some school systems/schools provide their own forms and require that teachers use them. The important point here is that you must take reasonable and prudent care to assure your students' safety and well being during a field trip.

Teacher(s) Arranging This Trip: _____

Destination: _____

Date Scheduled:_____ Alternative Date:_____

Classes Attending: _____

Number of Students Attending:_____ Adult/Student Ratio: _____

Travel Arrangements:_____

Educational Purpose: _____

_____

_____

Other Teachers Chaperoning: _____

_____

Chaperones (Parents and others at least 21 years of age): _____

_____

Names of Students not Attending (Attach a separate list if necessary.):

_____

Arrangements for Non-attendees care: _____

Time of departure:_____ Time of return:_____

* *

After School Hours Return Information

Arrangements for Transportation Home: _____

_____

Name of Teacher(s) to Monitor Students at School Until Transported Home

_____

Teacher Signature: _____

Date Submitted: _____

Index